"Erik Curren is onto the technology that may well win the future. And he is right that it is a patriotic quest. Winning clean energy independence would serve America very well indeed."

Bob Inglis
Former Congressman from South Carolina
Founder, RepublicEn

"If monopolistic utility lobbies are preventing the transition to clean energy in your state, this book is an excellent and practical guide for citizen advocacy and empowerment."

Marshall Saunders
Founder and President, Citizens' Climate Lobby

"Erik Curren has produced a solar-revolution manual that should inform, inspire, and energize anyone who believes in our inalienable right to a clean energy future."

Michael Brune
Executive Director, Sierra Club

"Curren parallels today's grassroots movements toward clean energy choices to the American colonists' struggles for freedom from tyranny. Renewable energy IS the new patriotism."

Mark Reynolds
Executive Director, Citizens' Climate Lobby

"The ability to use solar power at home helps keep your family more secure while helping America achieve a greater degree of energy independence. So, it's no wonder that support for solar and other clean energy is growing on the conservative side of the political spectrum. For conservatives and others who want to help their neighbors join America's clean energy revolution, *The Solar Patriot* is an indispensable source of good information and inspiration."

Mark Fleming
President & CEO, Conservatives for Clean Energy

"Democracy, patriotism, and rooftop solar go hand in hand and Erik Curren makes the case with simple, easy-to-understand stories from the front line of the modern-day battle for energy independence. Curren highlights parallels between today's fights and some of the most iconic stories from American history. This book is a great introduction to one of the most important issues of our time."

Anya Schoolman
Executive Director, Solar United Neighbors

"Everyone with an interest in solar, or who is a solar skeptic, should read this book. This is a highly engrossing call to arms for Solar Patriots, making insightful connections about freedom from electric utilities' efforts to control solar and our American Revolutionary heritage about seeking freedom from tyranny. The book informs as it engages the reader with vignettes about today's solar revolutionaries, and making the connections with the values, tactics, and leaders who won our American freedom. I would highly recommend this to anyone who seeks new insights on how solar represents an American ideal, combined with practical solutions on how to make a difference in making rooftop solar happen, either individually, or by finding common cause with a local or national group."

Anthony E. Smith, PhD
CEO and President, Secure Futures Solar

"Fighting for energy choice is much like arguments from Republicans around school or health care choice. It's about the free market and competition. It's about independence. It's about fighting for a better future. Giving people access to solar energy is one of the most patriotic things you can do. Erik Curren understands this concept and helps lay out an important vision in *The Solar Patriot*."

Tyson Grinstead
Director, Public Policy, Sunrun Inc.

"I loved this book. Curren is a fabulous writer and has a great story to tell. The solar revolution in this country is exciting, patriotic, and as vital to our future as the 1776 Revolution was to our past. This is that rare must-read

book for everyone, from liberal environmentalists to Tea Party conservatives."
Mike Tidwell
Director, Chesapeake Climate Action Network

"Today's generation of conservatives believes that we can enhance national security and promote economic growth at the same time as we protect the environment. The key is developing home-grown energy resources and clean technology. *The Solar Patriot* is a guidebook for young people and anyone else who wants to help ensure a prosperous economy now and for future generations of Americans."
Michele Combs
Founder and Chairman, Young Conservatives for Energy Reform

The Solar Patriot

The Solar Patriot

A Citizen's Guide to Helping America Win Clean Energy Independence

Erik Curren

New Sky Books

Cover design: Lindsay Curren

Published by New Sky Books, Staunton, Virginia.

Printed in the United States of America.

ISBN-13: 9780692976531
ISBN-10: 0692976531
Library of Congress Control Number: 2017916977
New Sky Books, Staunton, VA

Contents

Preface

To all brave, healthy, able bodied, and well-disposed young men, in this neighborhood, who have any inclination to join the troops now raising under GENERAL WASHINGTON, for the defense of the LIBERTIES AND INDEPENDENCE of the United States against the hostile designs of foreign enemies, TAKE NOTICE.

—Continental Army Recruiting Poster

In the eighteenth century, the American War of Independence was a violent but necessary revolution to bring freedom to this continent and, ultimately, to much of the world.

Today, the battle for clean energy independence will be a peaceful revolution, but one just as necessary to secure the future of America and the whole world.

In the spirit of the patriots of old, this book aims to recruit you as a champion for rooftop solar power. If you're a homeowner who already has installed solar panels on your roof or in your yard, this book is definitely for you. But the book will also be interesting to anyone who supports more solar power in America. I hope the book's approach will also be appealing to history buffs, among whom I count myself.

The Solar Patriot's method is unique but simple. The book connects the story of the American Revolution in the eighteenth century to today's fight for solar rights. Our fight today for clean energy independence is peaceful but it's just as urgent and just as crucial to America's future as the war fought by George Washington's soldiers two-and-a-half centuries ago.

Each chapter starts with an inspiring quote from one of the founders of our country to frame a discussion of each step on the journey towards empowering yourself as a solar patriot armed with the weapons of information and motivation. Then, each chapter ends with a classic story from the American Revolution with a key lesson for that stage of the solar patriot's journey.

The historic War for Independence pit American patriots against the British Empire of King George III. It was a David and Goliath battle where American backwoods farmers armed with old muskets defeated professional

British soldiers supplied with the most modern weapons and backed up by the world's most powerful navy.

Today's battle for solar rights pits solar homeowners and ordinary citizens who want America to use more solar power against monopoly electric utilities and fossil fuel companies that want to stop, or at least slow down, the spread of rooftop solar. This is also a David and Goliath contest where ordinary American families must stand up to some of the most powerful corporations in the history of the United States or the world.

Fighting to create a country where the rights of all people to life, liberty, and the pursuit of happiness would be respected, the Americans prevailed because history was on their side. In the Age of Enlightenment, the tide was turning against the forces of aristocracy and royalty and towards freedom and equality. Grit and commitment helped the patriots to prevail against stronger forces. And so did recruiting powerful allies like France and Spain.

In today's battle to make solar power America's leading energy source and to give ordinary Americans the right to make, use, sell, and share their own solar power, history is also clearly on our side. An energy source whose fuel is free of cost—sunshine—and produces no pollution is certain to prevail over coal, oil, natural gas, and nuclear power, all of which rely on dwindling fuel supplies and all of which create dangerous pollution or waste.

But the question for today's solar revolution is when solar will prevail. If it takes too long, America's economy could suffer irreparable damage as other countries take the lead on solar power. And if we cannot slow the rate of climate change, then America will suffer along with the rest of the world—perhaps we will suffer even more in an uncertain climate future, given the level of comfort that we've gotten used to.

Finally, even if solar does become America's leading energy source in time to save our economy and the world's climate, it makes a big difference who controls that solar. Will it be homeowners and small businesses, with millions of solar arrays on their rooftops, each a source of clean energy independence, greater national security, and resilience for the whole country? Or will monopoly electric utilities squeeze this new energy source into outdated centralized grid technology and a business model from the 1890s where they produce all the power themselves, leaving the rest of us vulnerable to grid failure and utility profit-seeking?

Patriots of the 1770s knew that the world was watching the battle in America between ordinary citizens and the mighty British Empire. And solar patriots today know that if America takes leadership on spreading rooftop solar now that the rest of the world will soon follow.

Consider this book a call to (peaceful) arms. An exciting and historic journey awaits you if you decide to enlist as a solar patriot. And just as we rightly celebrate the accomplishments of the American Revolutionaries in beating long odds to give the world a new birth of freedom in 1776, so I believe that generations yet unborn will celebrate today's solar patriots for giving our country and the rest of the world a new birth of prosperity.

Introduction

Our cause is noble. It is the cause of mankind!

—George Washington

Since you've picked up this book, I'm sure you're interested in solar power. You may already know that America is facing an energy crisis that's as much about the economy as it is about the environment. And you may feel that solar power is a key part of the solution.

But you may wonder about pairing up solar power with patriotism. So, let's talk about that a little.

Why Solar Needs Patriotism

Some people see patriotism as an important part of the American past that they can connect with today. As

Abraham Lincoln said, "I like to see a man proud of the place in which he lives. I like to see a man live so that his place will be proud of him."

But other people aren't as comfortable with the idea of patriotism. Indeed, my experience is that many of my friends who are most excited about solar power tend to agree with English writer Dr. Samuel Johnson's quip that, "Patriotism is the last refuge of a scoundrel." Or they may agree with Mark Twain's satirical definition, "Patriot: the person who can holler the loudest without knowing what he is hollering about." These friends talk more about saving the earth or fighting climate change to help the world than they talk about solar as a way to make America *itself* stronger.

But it's my premise that patriotism, a vigorous economy, a healthier planet, and the fight against climate chaos can go together for the benefit of us all.

In our country, patriotism is a powerful way to bring seemingly opposing issues together in a way that Americans with different political opinions can agree on today. One thing that I know we all agree about, whether we're conservative or progressive or independent, is that we want to make America a better place.

We may disagree on how to move our country forward. But that's part of what creates good ideas. This book will argue that solar power is one of the best ideas to improve America that everybody can get behind, no matter who you voted for in the last election.

For me, patriotism is simply about working for what's best for a person's own country.

Patriotism doesn't mean that you agree with the government on all things, whether war or peace. Patriotism also doesn't mean that trying to help your country means you don't care about people in other countries—or even other species that share the earth with humans. Patriotism just means that you want to start where you are and where you can make the most difference. "Think globally and act locally" as the bumper sticker says.

Across America and around the world, the most important group to most people outside of their family and local community is their country. Whatever our creed, color or career, it's our country, after all, whose language we speak, whose money we carry in our pockets, and whose history informs the values by which we live. Throughout our history, many Americans have died for those same values. Wherever you went to school, you probably learned these values as a kid. Historians usually identify several key values that Americans all share and that we have attempted to live our lives by for the last couple centuries and more.

According to *America: The Pocket Guide,* a booklet for use in schools put out by the educational arm of Colonial

Williamsburg, the key American values established after the Revolution come in pairs:

- Law vs Ethics
- Unity vs Diversity
- Common Wealth vs Private Wealth
- Freedom vs Equality

Sometimes we have to choose between these values and pick one side or the other. For example, we will usually decide to follow the law, even if we don't agree with it or if we think that a particular law is unethical.

A rigid mindset reminiscent of monarchies and dictatorships may come down on one side or the other of these values. For example, many Communist governments of the former Soviet Bloc chose to promote common wealth at the expense of private wealth. So, they confiscated land and investments of better off citizens to put the resources into services intended to benefit everybody. Unfortunately, despite good intentions, this didn't work out well. Rigid government never does.

By contrast, in America, a democratic mindset will always try to balance out competing values, for example, finding a way to increase both common wealth and private wealth. This book will argue that solar power is one of the most promising ways to do that, by helping the whole American economy to enjoy clean energy independence while making individual households more financially secure.

If you decide to become an advocate for rooftop solar power, as this book will invite you to do, then you'll join the effort to change laws affecting solar so that they match up more closely with ethical concerns. For example, it may be the law today in some states that electric utilities can charge solar homeowners extra fees every month just to stay connected to the electric grid. These fees can be so high that they discourage homeowners from getting solar panels installed at all. And that's not in the public interest. That's just crony capitalists—in this case, monopoly electric utilities—using their influence in government to protect their own industry against competition.

If you think this kind of discrimination is not fair, then I hope you'll join the movement to stand up for solar rights and get laws like this changed.

Lessons from the Past for A Solar Future

America has a long history of patriotic heroes whose stories have stood the test of time. Men and women of the past, especially those who fought in the American Revolution, were not perfect people. But they demonstrated vision and courage that can still inspire us even in the cynical age in which we live today.

In addition to looking at the challenges to rooftop solar now and talking about how to overcome those obstacles, this book will also tap into some of the most powerful stories from America's past to guide us as everyday solar advocates now.

I'm a history buff, and if you are too, then you'll get as much energy as I do by remembering how American patriots of the past triumphed against long odds. And if history wasn't your favorite subject in school, don't worry. This book will make stories from the American Revolution easy to follow. Not only will you get pumped up for solar power, but you'll also get a refresher on some basics of history that every American should know. I'm sure this will help you impress your friends and family. And knowing more about the founding of the country will also help you become a more confident citizen.

Most of all, this book will give you both the inspiration and the information you need to become an effective champion for solar power.

If you just want to help your friends and family follow your example and go solar themselves, you'll get advice on how to clearly explain the benefits that you get from solar in a way that they'll find compelling. Then, you'll get guidance on referring potential solar buyers to the installer who put up your solar system or another reputable solar installer.

If you want to help educate people and build support for rooftop solar, in this book you'll find a clear story about how solar can help America. You'll also find answers to the most common questions that people have about solar power along with a list of books that can help you learn more.

And if you're ready to take your work for solar to the next level, to support local, state, and federal laws that can help solar to spread, then you'll want to read the book's chapter on advocacy and lobbying. It's not as hard as you may think to influence public officials!

You may have ideas about lobbying already. For example, you may think that lobbying is a way that moneyed special interests bend government to support private profit. Or that lobbying only succeeds when done by high paid political operatives who wear Gucci loafers to work at plush offices on K Street in Washington, DC.

If this is your idea of lobbying, then you may be in for a surprise. Most of the people who visit elected officials are actually ordinary citizens representing their own concerns as volunteers. I know this from my own experience as a citizen who has lobbied for solar power in Washington, DC and in my state capital. I also know that citizen lobbying works from my other experience as an elected official, elected twice as a member of the city council of Staunton, Virginia, where I've lived for the last ten years.

Finally, I know that lobbying by ordinary citizens works because successful activists and experts who've studied government say that it's so. This book will quote some of those activists and experts to tell you how to do lobbying as a citizen most effectively.

Should you step up to the challenge to join your fellow Americans as a citizen lobbyist for solar power, this book will refer you to established groups that can help you get started. Or, if you prefer to do it yourself, you'll find tools to help you handle the whole process of advocacy and lobbying from crafting your simple pro-solar talking points to creating effective handouts to scheduling meetings with elected officials and following up with them afterwards.

Whatever level of commitment you're ready to make to helping spread solar in America, as a solar homeowner (or simply an apartment-dwelling solar friend), you're the exact right person at the exact right time to speak for solar today. With the environmental and economic challenges around energy that the world faces today, America needs you as a solar champion now more than ever.

You don't have to be an elected official yourself to help pass laws that promote solar power and repeal laws that block solar. Nor do you have to be a great leader in war, business, or sports to help make history in America today. Rooftop solar could make the difference for future generations. In this century, will America fall behind other nations that are going solar faster? Or will we continue to lead the world on innovation and prosperity for decades or even centuries to come?

You don't have to be at the head of an army to help win victory in this historic cause. You just have to show up and speak up.

As Robert Kennedy said, "Few will have the greatness to bend history itself; but each of us can work to change a small portion of events, and in the total of all those acts will be written the history of this generation."

From the Revolution: "The Cause of Mankind"

The quote from George Washington that opened this introduction comes from 1779, during the darkest days of the American Revolution. At that time, neither Washington nor anyone else could be sure that a set of backwoods colonies could throw off the greatest power on earth, the mighty British Empire, and establish a new kind of country, one dedicated to the value that everybody deserves a chance to succeed.

The American Revolution was partially a group of people looking out for their own interests, Americans who wanted to make their own decisions without interference from a king across the Atlantic. But the revolution was also something else, something bigger. It was a group of people trying to solve one of the world's oldest and biggest problems, namely, how to create a country where people of all kinds would have the best chance to live as they themselves choose.

America's cause did indeed turn out to be the cause of mankind. The vast majority of nations on earth today are not ruled by kings but instead by presidents and legislatures elected by their people. And those were all inspired by the work of the original American revolutionaries, from Washington and Jefferson to Adams and Hamilton.

Fast forward to the 21st century, and the world may not be perfectly democratic. But overall, the last two and a half centuries since the American Revolution have seen steady progress towards government by and for the people of every nation. At the same time, the nations of the world face a new problem. It's a problem as daunting as the challenge faced by Washington and the other founders of the United States. That problem is how to run modern civilization without dirty energy. And the solution is solar power.

Believe it or not, the amount of solar energy that hits the Earth in one hour could supply all the world's electricity needs for a whole year. Given that supplies of fossil fuels are limited and that using fossil fuels endangers our future, the cause of solar power is the cause of all mankind.

As the leading nation in the world, and its leading user of fossil fuels, if we can solve the problem of energy in America, then we can help the whole world to move forward to a clean energy future.

So, indeed, the cause of solar powering America is noble. It is also the cause of mankind everywhere.

One

The Attack on Rooftop Solar

It is the first responsibility of every citizen to question authority.

— Benjamin Franklin

Putting the Desert Sun to Good Use

When Pat and Craig Carrell got solar panels for their home in sunny Nevada, they wanted to save money and take control over their own energy. But they had no idea that their utility company would try to kill their solar dream.

After a career in higher education, Pat and Craig moved to a retirement community outside of Las Vegas in 2002. "The day we moved here, the temperature was 115 degrees, so that was a welcome to Nevada," Pat told *PBS NewsHour.*[1]

It turned out to be more expensive to retire in Nevada than Pat and Craig had expected. Each year, as summer came on and the thermometer crept past 100 degrees and then kept going up, the air conditioning had to work harder and harder. The couple's electric bills went through the roof. During the summer, Pat and Craig paid more than $450 per month for electricity.

To get costs under control, first the Carrells tried to get more efficient with the way they used energy. They added insulation to the attic and sun-blocking ultraviolet film to the windows. That helped some, but the Carrells' power bills were still high. They'd heard that Nevada was an excellent place to go solar, with more than 300 days a year of sun and strong state incentives. So, in 2014, they decided to get solar panels at home.

Pat and Craig invested $45,000 to hire a solar installer to put a solar array on the roof of their two-bedroom home. (Note: the price of solar panels has dropped greatly since then. Today, in most states, the average home can get a solar array that will meet most or all of its electricity needs for $15,000 or less). A solar tax credit from the federal government along with credits from their local utility company cut their initial cost by more than 40 percent. They expected the rest of the investment to pay for itself through lower electric bills over the next few years.

Once the couple's solar system went live, their strategy started to work just as they'd planned. On average, their bills dropped by about 95 percent, down to just $15 per month even in the hottest days of summer. Their bill was so low because the Carrells' solar panels made enough electricity to cover the couple's needs throughout the year.

Under Nevada's net metering law, they could sell the extra power their solar panels made during the day to their local utility at the full retail rate. In exchange, since they didn't choose to have a battery backup at home and remained connected to the electric grid, the utility would provide Pat and Craig power at night, when their solar panels weren't generating energy.

This was a good deal for everybody. The Carrells saved money and gained more energy independence. The clean power they produced helped reduce the need for dirty electricity from coal and other fossil fuels, cutting pollution for everybody. And they even helped the utility company by offering the company low-cost power during the hottest hours of the day when the utility would otherwise have to buy all its additional power at high prices on the "spot" market to meet high customer demand.

It was good news for Nevada's homeowners when solar grew 400 percent in the state between 2014 and 2015. It was also good news for the state's economy, as solar companies created thousands of new jobs, helping to lower the state's high unemployment rate. But then, dark clouds started to gather on the horizon.

The Empire Strikes Back

Nevada's biggest utility, NV Energy, didn't think that more solar in Nevada was good news. They just saw that solar panels were allowing good customers like the Carrells to make their own energy at home and stop using centralized power controlled and distributed by NV Energy. That kind of competition from rooftop solar could eat into the utility's profits in the future.

As SolarCity's Marco Krapels explained to *PBS NewsHour*,

> Now solar is becoming real. The utility monopolies are saying, "Well wait a minute, we've got to crush it before it gets too big."
>
> They want to build more plants so they can make more money, and if we take a little bite out of that apple, and we say, "Hey guys, we've got solar panels everywhere on all these homes, you don't need to build them any more power plants," then the utility goes, "Well, wait a minute, how am I going to make more money next year?"

So, to protect its own business, the utility company decided to strike back at solar.

Employing high-paid lobbyists and using their massive political influence, NV Energy managed to get Nevada's laws changed to punish people who already had solar at home and scare away anyone else who might think of getting solar in the future.

The utility attack on solar worked. In December of 2015, after heavy lobbying from NV Energy, Nevada's three-member Public Utilities Commission decided to triple the fee they allow the utility to charge rooftop solar owners just to stay connected to the grid—from $12.75 a month, to more than $38 a month. The Commission also decided that the utility company no longer needed to credit solar customers at the retail rate for electricity, the same rate that those customers would pay to buy energy from the utility. Instead, the utility company would only buy power from solar homeowners at a lower "wholesale" rate of 75 percent off.

And worst of all for homeowners like Pat and Craig Carrell, the change was retroactive. They weren't grandfathered in for the life of their solar system at the current rates. Instead, in the future, they would now have to pay a higher monthly fee to the utility while taking a big cut in solar payments. This meant that most of the savings that they'd counted on getting from solar would now be taken away. And 17,000 other homeowners who had gone solar in the state would now also see their savings from solar taken away by NV Energy.

As Pat Carrell explained, "It's not the rules that we bought into, they changed the game on us. That was hard-earned savings, but we decided it was worth it to put it up on our roof, to have that kind of energy independence, and now it seems like it's gone."

The change in solar rates practically killed the solar industry in Nevada overnight. New orders for solar installations dropped to nearly zero. All three of the largest national installers announced that they'd be closing their operations in Nevada, resulting in layoffs for hundreds of solar workers.

Fortunately, the story doesn't end here. Solar homeowners got angry and helped lead a movement to bring back favorable rates for Nevada solar. And in the spring of 2017, the pro-solar coalition achieved success when the Nevada state legislature voted to reinstate net metering at nearly the retail rate. We'll talk about that more later.

Yet, Nevada was only one battlefield in monopoly utilities' war on rooftop solar. Utilities had a battle plan to bring the fight to the rest of the country too, starting with another sunny state perfect for solar—the Sunshine State itself. The next chapter will talk about the secret strategy that utilities hoped would kill the rooftop solar revolution in the state of Florida.

From the Revolution: Taxation without Representation

Even before the American Revolution, the thirteen British colonies on the Atlantic seaboard prided themselves on a tradition of self-governance that went back to their founding documents, such as the Mayflower Compact in Massachusetts and the charter of the Virginia Company. But this tradition would be tested when their British rulers needed cash.

After the French and Indian War ended in 1763, the British government was deeply in debt. To pay off expenses incurred during the war, during the 1760s and 1770s King George III and Parliament imposed a series of taxes on Americans. Taxing the colonies was popular in Britain because it allowed the government to reduce land taxes back home. It all started in 1765 with the Stamp Act, which required a paid tax stamp on colonial newspapers, legal documents, and even playing cards. And it ended nearly a decade later with the tax on the Americans' tea. These taxes were not high. But they angered the colonists because the taxes were imposed from England without the colonists' participation.

Previously, the colonists had been used to only paying taxes that they decided to levy on themselves. If the colonists agreed to pay the new taxes imposed from the outside, they would be admitting that British authorities had a right to take the colonists' money without their consent, since Americans had no representatives in Parliament. Also, since Britons back home didn't have to pay these taxes, the Americans, who considered themselves equal to people living in Britain, thought that these taxes discriminated against the colonies. So, to demand fairness and to protect their autonomy, the colonists protested the taxes.

Today, solar homeowners are not facing additional taxes *per se*. But solar homeowners are facing additional fees from utilities approved by state governments, as in the case of Nevada. Yet, the parallel between these government-approved utility fees on solar today and the taxes imposed by the British government on the American colonists before the Revolution is clear.

Monopoly utilities are a kind of private company that has power similar to that of a government. When such a utility levies an extra fee on solar homeowners without the consent of either the homeowners or local citizens, then that utility is acting like an autocratic power. To protect their rights, solar homeowners have begun to stand up to utilities and to the government regulators and elected officials who help those utilities to deprive solar homeowners of their private property without giving them adequate representation in the decision-making process.

Two

The Secret Plan to Quell the Rooftop Rebellion

Justly those we tyrants call who
the body would enthrall.
Tyrants of more cruel kind—those
who would enslave the mind.

"Cupid, God of Soft Persuasion"
(18th Century song)

It turns out that the attack on rooftop solar in Nevada wasn't an isolated skirmish. It was actually part of a secret plan by the utility industry to kill, or at least slow down, rooftop solar around America. And in the sunny state of Florida, this plan almost worked to fool citizens who overwhelmingly supported solar power into voting against their own right to go solar at home.

This plan, concocted by a cartel of monopoly utility companies trying to protect themselves from competition by rooftop solar, was revealed to the public by watchdog groups who obtained documents presented at utility industry meetings. The watchdogs then shared the utilities' private plan with the news media. This plan involved nothing less than trying to alter the English language itself.

The strategy was to change the meaning of common terms having to do with energy and inventing new ones to make utilities look like trusted advisors with the public's best interest at heart. At the same time, the language change would try to make rooftop solar companies and customers appear greedy, self-centered, and shady.

The goal? To turn the public against rooftop solar. That would put rooftop solar installers on the defensive and place utilities back in the driver's seat. If successful, this plan could put many rooftop solar installers out of business and slow down the spread of rooftop solar across America.

Orwellian Newspeak

To understand the strategy behind the utilities' plan to deceive the public about rooftop solar, let's take a quick detour into the world of literature. Perhaps you'll remember that in George Orwell's dystopian novel of a totalitarian future, *Nineteen Eighty-Four*, the government of fictional Oceana took control of the language that ordinary people spoke in order to control the way people think.[2] That kind of brainwashing made it easier for the repressive government of Big Brother to control how people behaved.

Really, by getting inside people's minds, Big Brother got people to become their own oppressors.

So, in the name of simplifying things—for example, replacing the word "better" with the phrase "plusgood" or putting words together like "Newspeak" (new + speak)—Big Brother's regime changed the meaning of words to suit its needs. For example:

- "Free thinking" became "crimethink," meaning that thinking for yourself was now illegal.
- Likewise, "brainwashed" became "goodthink," meaning that if you accepted the government's point of view on all things without question, you were a good citizen.

Big Brother's rule also relied on double-think, which is basically the ability to believe lies, even if they're obvious, as long as they come from Big Brother. Examples are the three slogans of Big Brother's political party, *War is Peace*, *Freedom is Slavery*, and *Ignorance is Strength*.

As a way to help kill rooftop solar, for the last few years, the trade association for monopoly utilities, the

Edison Electric Institute, has been pushing a version of Orwell's Newspeak applied to the energy industry.

The EEI represents investor-owned utilities around the U.S., including companies in the Southeast such as Dominion, Duke, Appalachian Power, the Southern Company, and Florida Public Utilities. That's important because activists have identified the region as the sunniest part of the country with the least amount of solar but with the biggest potential for more solar because of good sunshine.

And why do sunny southeastern states like Georgia or Florida have so little solar compared to more northerly states like New York or Massachusetts? You can't blame it on the sun. The real problem is state rules and regulations that discriminate against rooftop solar. Even as citizens demanded more solar power, states enacted anti-solar public policy and kept it in force largely due to the influence of local utilities in each state. And those utilities got valuable help trying to kill rooftop solar from the Edison Electric Institute.

In 2014, at a private meeting of utilities in Las Vegas, the EEI rolled out its plan to change the way that the English language talks about energy. Called the Lexicon Project, the plan began in secret, though it was later leaked to the Huffington Post and other news media in 2016.[3]

In the Lexicon Project, just like Big Brother in Orwell's novel, utilities say they want to simplify communication. "We're trying to communicate more simply, in a more understandable language, but in a way that also reflects this fundamental change in how we want the industry to be viewed going forward," explained Dale Heydlauff, vice president for corporate communications at American Electric Power Co.

That sounds harmless enough. But this effort has dark implications for rooftop solar. Just check out a few of the words about solar that utilities want to replace, according to a report by their consultant Maslansky + Partners, published in full on the website UtilitySecrets.org and summarized by the Institute for Local Self-Reliance, an advocacy group that supports rooftop solar and other local renewable energy[4]:

Current Usage	**Utility Newspeak**
Utility-scale solar	Universal solar
Rooftop solar	Private solar
Solar installation	Solar power plant
Distributed generation	Private generation (where appropriate)
Net metering	Private solar credits
Wholesale rate	Competitive rate
Baseload generation	24/7 power sources

My favorite here is changing "rooftop solar" into "private solar." Just think about it. That makes it sound selfish to put solar panels on your roof instead of just buying more expensive "green power" from your local utility's large solar plant that may not even offer power for your particular home or business.

Take another example of dangerous utility propaganda. If policymakers start thinking of net metering as "private solar credits," then homeowners getting paid for the clean energy that PV panels on their roof produce starts to sound like just another government handout to special interests.

Also, the Lexicon Project advises utilities to use the word "smart" more often, as it polled well with the public in their research. More on that below.

Having compiled its biased word list, the utility lobby is not just sitting back and waiting for people to discover it. No, they're actively encouraging everybody they can to start adopting their new language, as energy and environment publication E&E News explains[5]:

> Berkshire Hathaway Energy Co. [the parent of Nevada's utility NV Energy, mentioned in the last chapter] already is incorporating the lexicon into its communications, said Julie White, vice president for corporate communications at the holding company. The transition to a new way of talking about its business has been "fairly smooth," she

said, underscoring the importance of explaining the research behind the language to executives.

After adopting its list of Orwellian terms to make rooftop solar look bad, the Edison Electric Institute started a program to train the employees of its member companies to use this new language, using webinars and other Internet-based tools.

Then, EEI began reaching out to the trade associations for electric cooperatives and municipal utilities, sharing the research in the hopes that their anti-rooftop solar language would be adopted industrywide. If utilities can get people outside of their own employees to start using their energy Newspeak, imagine how easy it will be for the utility lobby to push back solar-friendly policies like net metering in any state.

And that's exactly what they tried to do in Florida in 2016.

In Florida, where "Smart" Meant "Dumb"

A cartel of monopoly utilities including Florida Power & Light, Duke Energy Florida, Gulf Power, and Tampa Electric pushed the deceptively named "Smart Solar" initiative on the November 2016 Florida statewide ballot.

Using completely Orwellian language, the group claimed the initiative would promote "solar choice" by adding an amendment to the state's constitution claiming to give Floridians the "right" to get solar—while also opening the door for more regulation of the industry.

This language was deceptive for several reasons.

According to Florida Supreme Court Justice Barbara Pariente, Sunshine State residents already had the right to get solar. But if the amendment passed, utility companies could have used it to block competition from solar installers by claiming they are insufficiently regulated or that rooftop solar somehow imposes a subsidy on non-solar utility customers.

Pariente was one of many experts in law and public policy who warned Florida citizens about this solar wolf-in-sheep's clothing:

> Let the pro-solar energy consumers beware. Masquerading as a pro-solar energy initiative, this proposed constitutional amendment, supported by some of Florida's major investor-owned electric utility companies, actually seeks to constitutionalize the status quo. The ballot title is affirmatively misleading by its focus on "Solar Energy Choice," when no real choice exists for those who favor expansion of solar energy.

When you use the word "choice" to mean "less choice," the implications of Orwellian language for public policy are clear.

Freedom = Slavery, anyone?

Leading up to the election, utilities spent $26 million on ads and even set up a fake citizen's group, Consumers for Smart Solar, to push for the initiative.

For intrigue, the story of the secret utility plan behind this deceptive ballot measure matches any of the spy stories from the American Revolution found in the 2006 book *Washington's Spies: The Story of America's First Spy Ring* by Alexander Rose, later made into a gripping TV series by AMC.

During the American Revolution, spies reporting directly to George Washington uncovered British battle plans and covert operations alike, helping the Americans to outmaneuver a much stronger foe. In the same way, just before the election of 2016, a couple of watchdog groups in Florida allied with solar advocates to expose plans by the state's largest electric utilities to deceive Florida voters into voting to restrict the spread of rooftop solar.

For months leading up to the election, the pro-solar forces had claimed that the utilities' ballot initiative, Amendment 1, was deceptive. And in October, two watchdog groups seemed to confirm that the initiative was a deliberate utility plot to deceive voters when they made an audio recording available to the *Miami Herald*.[6]

The audio recorded an industry consultant called Sal Nuzzo explaining to a private meeting of utility industry executives that Amendment 1 was "an incredibly savvy maneuver" that "would completely negate anything they (pro-solar interests) would try to do either legislatively or constitutionally down the road."

In other words, if Amendment 1 passed, it would be difficult for pro-solar rules and regulations to be put in place in Florida in the future.

Nuzzo reminded his audience that ordinary citizens strongly support solar power: "As you guys look at policy in your state, or constitutional ballot initiatives in your state, remember this: Solar polls very well," he said.

The consultant then went on to flatter the Florida utility executives at the meeting for being so clever with the wording of Amendment 1 as to wrap an anti-solar wolf in pro-solar sheep's clothing:

> "To the degree that we can use a little bit of political *jiu-jitsu* and take what they're kind of pinning on us and use it to our benefit either in policy, in legislation, or in constitutional referendums—if that's the direction you want to take—use the language of promoting solar, and kind of, kind of put in these protections for consumers that choose not to install rooftop."

Of course, by "protections for consumers that choose not to install rooftop," Nuzzo was really talking about protections for utilities against their customers defecting from their local utility by getting solar at home. While utilities claimed in Florida in 2016 (and continue to claim around the country today) that allowing solar customers to sell power back to the grid actually costs non-solar customers more money, solar advocates in Florida presented a report published in May 2016 by the Brookings Institution that effectively refuted this utility claim.[7]

According to the Brookings report and several other reports about solar net metering done in various states, the reality was the opposite: distributed solar provides value worth more to the grid than what solar homeowners are paid for their excess power through net metering.

Clean power sold back to the grid by rooftop solar owners helps non-solar customers by reducing the need to build new power plants, cutting demand for fossil fuels to generate power, and reducing the need for expensive maintenance on the grid. All that helps lower utility rates and increase energy security, saving utility customers money and giving them more reliable power, even if they don't use solar themselves.

As the Brookings report concluded, "The economic benefits of net metering actually outweigh the costs and impose no significant cost increase for non-solar customers.

Far from a net cost, net metering is in most cases a net benefit — for the utility and for non-solar rate-payers."

After the recording of consultant Sal Nuzzo's remarks about Amendment 1 was released in the middle of October, public support for the utility-sponsored ballot measure dropped drastically. And by the time election day came on November 8, the deceptive initiative failed to get the 60% of votes required under Florida's constitution to become law.

It was solar patriots from across the political spectrum who won this victory. Under the umbrella of Floridians for Solar Choice, a diverse coalition of 200 grassroots groups including solar companies along with both environmentalists and the Florida Tea Party, helped citizens to see the truth that Amendment 1 would set back the cause of solar in the Sunshine State by decades.

"Today, as a coalition representing every part of Florida's political spectrum, we defeated one of the most egregious and underhanded attempts at voter manipulation in this state's history," said Tory Perfetti, who served as both chairman of Floridians for Solar Choice and as director of Conservatives for Energy Freedom, in a statement. "We won against all odds and secured a victory for energy freedom."

Despite all the myth-busting of the pro-solar forces, many Florida voters were still fooled by the utilities' propaganda campaign. More than 4.5 million Floridians, accounting for 50.8 percent of all voters, actually voted in favor of Amendment 1. Clearly, though the utilities' campaign wasn't good enough to get the 60 percent of votes it needed to make Amendment 1 law, it was enough to deceive a majority of good citizens in Florida to vote against their own desire for more rooftop solar.

Solar Must Fight Back with Its Own Language

The Florida vote may have been a victory for rooftop solar in 2016, but it was not the end of the utilities' strategy to protect their monopoly by trying to confuse the public with tricky language. Just as the utility industry's Lexicon Project's Orwellian Newspeak helped deceive voters and policymakers in Florida when it was put into legislation in the form of Amendment 1, so the utility industry's devil's dictionary could also help utilities crush competition for solar among consumers in other states and on the federal level in the future.

If things go well for utilities and their language games, pretty soon solar installers can expect their potential customers to start asking about whether "private solar" (i.e., a rooftop array) is really right for them, or if they should just wait for "universal solar" from their utility.

After all, if solar is about doing the right thing, then who wants to be selfish and hog all the solar for themselves?

If homeowners and business owners start to believe utility propaganda, it could be disastrous for rooftop solar.

Nick Stumo-Langer of the Institute for Local Self-Reliance suggests that the solar industry should offer its own list of word changes to put utilities in their place. He's got a handy and entertaining list:

Instead of...	Use...
Utility	Incumbent monopoly
Fixed charge	Monopoly protection fee
Cost-shift	Non-monopoly benefits
Baseload generation	Inflexible generation

It would be more accurate for solar homeowners to adopt Stumo-Langer's list when they talk to their family, friends, and neighbors and elected officials alike. But more importantly, anyone who supports rooftop solar should not be intimidated by the utility lobby's campaign to corrupt the English language.

If anyone was being selfish in Florida's battle over Amendment 1, it was not solar homeowners. It was really the opposite. Homeowners who invested their own money to install solar panels on their rooftops and sold their excess energy back to the grid were the ones helping their neighbors to enjoy some of the benefits of clean solar energy. The selfish ones in this case were the electric utilities who put their own profits ahead of the wellbeing of Florida's citizens while seeking to deceive the public into voting against their own desire for more solar.

We all need to stand up for the integrity of words used to talk about energy and do our part to educate the people we know with the truth about rooftop solar—that it's one of the most patriotic ways to help America today. That's what the next chapter will discuss.

From the Revolution: The Arrogance of King George III

Someday, given the distance between Britain and America, it was inevitable that Britain's thirteen colonies from New England to Georgia would want their independence. But it was the actions of King George III (reigned 1760-1820) that caused Americans to revolt in the second half of the 18th century and ultimately led to American independence in 1776.

The trouble began when the British started imposing taxes on Americans to buy items ranging from lead to paper to tea. These taxes were not imposed on people in Britain. Even worse, the new duties passed without the Americans' consent, as we saw in the previous chapter. To protect their freedoms, at first, Americans sought redress from these imposed taxes, sending respectful petitions to the King. But as George III's government imposed ever more taxes and then came up with other ways to extract revenue from the colonies such as quartering troops in private homes, Americans turned to rebellion against imperial rule.

Encouraged by hardline advisors such as Prime Minister Lord Frederick North, the headstrong George III refused to compromise with the colonists. When the Americans published the Declaration of Independence in 1776, they didn't just blame the British government, but they blamed the King specifically for their grievances. "The history of the present King of Great Britain is a history of repeated injuries and usurpations, all having in direct object the establishment of an absolute tyranny over these states."

One of the grievances against George III mentioned in the Declaration of Independence was sending foreign mercenaries—the Hessians whom Washington would beat at the Battle of Trenton after crossing the Delaware—to "complete the works of death, desolation, and tyranny… totally unworthy of the head of a civilized nation." In the same way, in 2016, electric utilities in Florida used the front group Consumers for Smart Solar to do their dirty work for them in convincing voters through deception that the anti-solar Amendment 1 was actually good for solar.

In the end, George III wouldn't compromise with the Americans, and yet he wasn't able to muster enough force to suppress the colonists' revolt against imperial rule either. In the same way, the momentum behind solar power is so great today that no cabal of monopoly utilities can stop solar from becoming America's top energy source at some point.

But using their money to fool the public and influence government, utilities can certainly slow down rooftop solar for decades. Yet, in coming years, when solar + battery storage becomes more affordable, homeowners can simply defect from the electric grid, perhaps even putting utilities out of business. That means utilities now have a choice. They can compromise with solar homeowners and find a way to make peace. Or, they can continue to fight rooftop solar, and risk losing their control over America's electricity system altogether, meeting much the same fate as King George III, whose stubbornness helped him to lose his American empire.

Three

Why Solar is Patriotic

There is a certain enthusiasm in liberty, that makes human nature rise above itself, in acts of bravery and heroism.

—Alexander Hamilton

If you accept that patriotism is a love for the place where you live that always tries to make that place better, then it's easy to see how helping to spread solar power around the country is one of the most patriotic things you can do for America today.

Everybody knows that America has an energy problem. No matter how cheap they may be today, prices for the fossil fuels that provide most of our energy have been high in the past. And they're certain to go up in the future. But even while energy is relatively cheap, getting that energy from fossil fuels hurts America in many ways. Replacing dirty energy with clean solar power increases America's security, health, and independence on every level. Just as solar gives our nation freedom from foreign energy sources, so solar also gives families freedom from control by monopoly electric utilities.

Solar Fights Climate Change

Burning fossil fuels including coal, oil, and natural gas makes climate change worse. Hotter temperatures have already led to flooding in coastal areas, stronger storms, drought in some places, and flooding in others. Climate change may not have *caused* hurricanes and storms like Katrina that devastated New Orleans in 2005 and the hurricanes that hit in 2017, including Harvey that flooded Houston, and Maria that wiped out infrastructure including the electric grid in Puerto Rico. But climate change made those storms *stronger and deadlier*.

In the future, the effects of climate change on Americans will vary by state, and will be felt most strongly by low-income families and children, the elderly, and others vulnerable to heat stroke and tropical diseases that will start to expand into northerly areas.

This book isn't going to go over climate science, so if you don't believe in climate change you're welcome to skip down to the next heading. But if you happen to be someone who considers yourself a conservative and if you have doubted climate science in the past, then I hope you'll consider this story. It's about a conservative leader who used to think that climate science was a hoax but later changed his mind.

Like most of his Republican colleagues at the time, former South Carolina Congressman Bob Inglis worried that solutions to climate change would hurt the economy, so he simply dismissed the science. Then, after some time out of Congress, in 2003 Inglis decided to get back into politics and run for his old seat.

By now, his son Rob had reached voting age, but he gave his dad a shock when he said that he couldn't take his son's support for granted in the future. "Dad, I'll vote for you, but you have got to clean up your act on the environment."

All four of Rob's sisters agreed. So did Inglis' wife Mary Anne.

Inglis took his family seriously as a constituency, and so he decided to dig deeper into the issue of climate. As it turned out, his research went far beyond doing a few Google searches.

In the next few years, Inglis wound up on a couple trips to Antarctica to see ice-core data and saw that carbon dioxide, the main greenhouse gas, was at steady levels for millennia until it showed a sharp rise in the Industrial

Revolution. He even went scuba diving off the Great Barrier Reef, viewing devastating coral bleaching with an Australian climate scientist who shared Inglis' religious faith and love for God's creation.

After that, the conservative Congressman became convinced that climate change was real, that it was a major threat both to the environment and to civilization, and that humans were the main cause. That's when Inglis became an advocate for climate solutions. He even introduced a bill to Congress, the Raise Wages, Cut Carbon Act of 2009, that would impose a carbon tax on fossil fuels and then use the proceeds to reduce taxes for families hard hit by the recession. Inglis' legislation didn't go anywhere in Congress. But unfortunately, his support for climate solutions did hurt him with voters back home when he ran for reelection in 2010. At some town hall meetings, people booed when he tried to talk. Inglis lost to challenger Trey Gowdy in a runoff election by 71 to 29 percent.

But Inglis was not discouraged. After leaving Congress, he founded RepublicEn, a group for conservatives who accept climate science and support free-market solutions. One of those solutions, a fee on carbon, would make it more expensive for fossil fuels to emit carbon into the atmosphere, and would make clean energy cheaper by comparison. Inglis thinks this is the best way to spread solar power, as he explained to me:

> The most powerful incentive is going to come when there are economic reasons apparent from our power meters as to why solar makes sense. That's when it's going to really take off. Of course, what we're talking about there is a price on carbon dioxide so we see the true cost of energy. And then we'll see that consumers will pursue their self-interest and they'll be dialing solar installers without anybody telling them what to do. It's going to change the way we do electricity in this country.

As Bob Inglis discovered, the bad news is that climate change doesn't care if you're progressive or conservative. Heat, storms, sea-level rise, and disease will affect all Americans at one time and place or another. The good news is that solar power is a climate solution for everybody—progressives, conservatives, and everyone else.

Solar Boosts the Economy

Even as the economy goes up and down, too many Americans still lack the good jobs that would allow them to enjoy the American Dream of homeownership and financial security for their families. After big manufacturers began outsourcing jobs in the 1970s, few of those jobs have returned to American towns and cities. More recently, companies have kept their plants here but have replaced workers with robots and more automation. The trend towards automation is sure to continue in the future.

Fortunately, solar is stepping in to help. Jobs in the solar industry grew 17 times faster than the American economy as a whole in 2017, according to the International Renewable Energy Agency.

Most solar workers install solar panels on the rooftops of homes, businesses, and government buildings. Other solar jobs are found in sales and marketing, product development, and engineering. Overall, these days, there are twice as many people working in the solar industry as in the whole coal industry. Even though coal still provides more of America's energy than solar does, these days coal requires fewer workers than in the past. To save money on labor costs, over the last fifty years, coal companies have replaced workers with machines to do jobs like mining and processing coal. As a result of this automation, 40 percent of coal jobs have disappeared since 2011.

Meanwhile, solar is labor intensive, and jobs like installing solar panels on a roof cannot be automated. And while most solar panels are manufactured abroad in China and other countries, installing solar panels on a roof is a job that must be done on site and can't be sent to a foreign country. Even some unemployed coal miners have gotten jobs as solar installers. Job training programs along the lines of Solar Ready Colorado, established in Delta County, an area where closed coal mines led to high unemployment, are popping up all over the country to help miners, oil workers, and even military veterans transition to careers in solar.

Paying $20 an hour or more, solar jobs are attractive for many workers. "It seems to be one of the few areas of high-paying, blue-collar jobs — and you don't have to learn to code," Bryan Birsic, CEO of Wunder Capital, told CNN Money.

Solar Gives America Energy Independence

While some of America's traditional energy sources, such as coal, are domestic, one of our most crucial energy sources today relies heavily on imports—oil.

Even as more people have gone solar at home and the solar industry has created more jobs, four decades after the energy crisis of the 1970s, America continues to depend on the same countries in the Middle East to provide much of our crude oil. Some people don't think there's anything that solar power can do about that, since most solar power provides electricity but most oil is used for transportation. After all, you can't fill up the tank of your gasoline car with electricity. Of course, if you have an electric car, it's a different story. That's where solar comes in. But first, let's talk about the problem of America depending on foreign oil.

Middle Eastern countries such as Saudi Arabia, Iraq, and Iran are breeding grounds for terrorists seeking to attack the United States. Ironically, much of the funding for terrorist training and operations in the Middle East comes from the very oil that Americans buy to run our cars, trucks, and airplanes. It's a tragic fact that, in buying Middle Eastern oil, Americans are unintentionally paying people who want to do us harm. It's much the same situation in other countries like Nigeria or Venezuela that also supply oil to the United States. We send them billions of dollars a year for oil, and some of that money always seems to find its way into the hands of dictators, radical political groups, and violent religious extremists who recruit young men with the slogan "Death to America!"

When the United States is dependent on foreign oil, then there's always a chance that our country will get tangled up in conflicts like the two wars in Iraq or even suffer another energy crisis like that of the 1970s. The last time energy prices spiked, in 2007 and 2008, our country faced the Great Recession where millions of workers lost jobs and families lost homes in communities across the nation.

Oil, coal, and nuclear power companies offer their own solutions for America to achieve energy independence. These ideas, which involve using more of their product, might be good for their CEOs and shareholders. But they're bad for America in many ways.

Well, we've heard plenty of big talk from the dirty energy industry about producing more fossil fuels at home, especially coal and natural gas. But since fossil fuels create so much pollution and because their supply is limited, doing more mining and drilling domestically is not a long-term solution to make the United States energy independent or to make America a better, healthier place to live for its citizens. Coal is on its way out just because other energy sources are more affordable. And natural gas is more polluting than the industry would have us believe. With methane gas leaks at gas wells, natural gas has turned out to be as polluting as coal.

The biggest non-fossil fuel option, nuclear power, has always been dangerous to operate, and plagued by unmanaged radioactive waste that will last centuries. And despite a short-lived nuclear "renaissance" over the last few years, now it's become too expensive to build new nuclear plants, with most new projects put on hold or cancelled outright. Once touted as able to produce electricity that would be "too cheap to meter," today, additional nuclear power would not be able to compete on price with solar and wind.

Now, back to oil. In the United States, 70 percent of all oil is used for transportation. This means that, if we can start to run more of America's vehicles on electricity powered by solar, then we can greatly cut down our use of oil, especially foreign oil.

The growth of electric vehicles powered by solar could end all growth in demand for not just coal but also oil around the world by 2020, according to researchers at Imperial College in London.[8] Meanwhile, other researchers predict that one out of three American cars, trucks, vans, and buses could be electric by 2030. Major automakers have started making and selling electric vehicles with a sticker price comparable to the cost of a gasoline car.

Battery technology is rapidly improving, with new model electric vehicles able to run for 200 miles or more on a single charge. And some car companies, including General Motors and Volvo, have pledged to phase out gasoline and diesel cars altogether and start making only electric cars in the future.

Solar Makes the Electric Grid More Resilient

In the spirit of patriotism, solar is as good for America's electric grid as it is for individual households. The electric grid of poles, wires, and other equipment needed to move electricity from where it's produced to where it's used is essential to provide the power that homes and businesses need every hour of every day to run modern civilization. But this grid is vulnerable to many threats, from damage in storms to attacks by hackers and terrorists.

The Hill newspaper outlined a "nightmare scenario" if the grid went down[9]:

> Stores are closed. Cell service is failing. Broadband Internet is gone.
>
> Hospitals are operating on generators, but rapidly running out of fuel.
>
> Garbage is rotting in the streets, and clean water is scarce as people boil water stored in bathtubs to stop the spread of bacteria.
>
> And escape?
>
> There is none, because planes can't fly, trains can't run, and gas stations can't pump fuel.

For something so important, the electric grid is surprisingly vulnerable to threats both big and small. Start with trees. On a hot day, power lines can sag and make contact with a nearby tree branch, causing an increase in current that can lead to a cascading failure that can produce a blackout in a local area. Overgrown trees around power lines were one of the causes of the Northeast Blackout of 2003 that shut down power for 55 million people in eight eastern U.S. states and the Canadian province of Ontario.

A software bug was another cause of that blackout. Unfortunately, the software that runs the electric grid is especially vulnerable to bugs since it's both complex and old—much of its code was written decades ago. Aging utility software is vulnerable to bugs and human error of operators. It's also vulnerable to a malicious attack by terrorists.

This is not a movie scenario, but something that has happened in real life. In 2015 hackers associated with the Russian government made a coordinated attack on the power grid of neighboring Ukraine, cutting electricity to a quarter million people. Since then, hacker attacks on Ukraine's grid have continued. China, Iran, North Korea, and even the terrorist group ISIS may also have malware capable of attacking America's electrical grid.

The U.S. grid would be harder to take down than the grid in Ukraine or other nations, experts say, but our electric grid would also be harder to bring back up once it's down. In the event of a major attack on the grid, large portions of the country could experience power outages for days, weeks, or even longer. The grid remains the most popular target for foreign hackers in the whole American economy according to *LIGHTS OUT: A Cyberattack, A Nation Unprepared, Surviving the Aftermath*, a book published in 2015 by veteran journalist Ted Koppel.

Yet cybersecurity experts quoted by Koppel say that federal authorities and electric utilities are not taking cyber threats to the grid seriously enough.

It's easy for hackers to target the software that runs the grid since the hackers just have to get into one of several dozen large computers around the country to get access to the whole grid for several states. In the same way, it's easy for terrorists to target major utility infrastructure like natural gas plants or electrical substations, because those centralized facilities are easy to find. And terrorists only need to attack one centralized facility to create major havoc for millions of households and businesses. That's the problem with the traditional centralized electricity system that developed in the United States starting in the nineteenth century. Antiquated grid and power generation technology still in operation leaves the power grid vulnerable to hacker and terrorist attacks today.

Fortunately, there's an easy solution to make America's electricity system more resilient—rooftop solar power. Distributed on rooftops and in backyards all over the country, thousands of small solar arrays make difficult targets for terrorists. And even when distributed solar arrays are connected to the grid, modern software renders them a much less attractive target to hackers than a big centralized computer at a utility company office running on legacy software from the 1980s.

As to the ordinary threat to the grid from heavy demand, rooftop solar is also a promising solution. Solar produces the most electricity just when demands for power on the grid are at their highest—on hot summer afternoons when businesses and homes are blasting their air conditioning. Solar that's connected to the grid steps in with extra power when it's needed most. This extra power helps keep costs down and prevents blackouts.

Unfortunately, electric utilities don't usually reward or even recognize the value of solar to the grid. Even worse, utilities often try to punish homeowners for getting solar by assessing a "standby charge" or other fee just to stay connected to the grid that only solar owners have to pay. Utilities claim that since solar homeowners buy little or no power from the grid during the day while still using the grid as their source of power at night, solar owners are getting a service that they're not paying for. That makes solar homeowners free riders whose costs must be covered by other utility customers who don't have solar, according to utilities.

But, as we saw from the Brookings Institution Report mentioned in the previous chapter, this just isn't true. Solar homeowners actually give much more back to the electric grid than they get out of it.

Just take one example from a sunny state with a lot of homes that have solar, Arizona. For every dollar that solar customers cost the utility company Arizona Public Service, those solar homeowners provide $1.54 worth of value to other customers of the utility. That's because solar homeowners offer their neighbors several important benefits, according to a study by the Solar Energy Industries Association:

> Benefits include savings on expensive and polluting conventional power and power plants; reduced investments in transmission and distribution infrastructure; reduced electricity lost during

transportation over power lines, as distributed solar power is generated and consumed locally; and savings on the cost of meeting renewable energy requirements.

Solar homeowners are not free riders on the electric grid. Instead, they're the patriots who have invested their own money to help make the grid more resilient for everybody, all while saving their neighbors money.

Solar Makes Families More Resilient

For most American families, their electricity bill is their second highest monthly expense at home after their mortgage or rent. Solar can save families large amounts of money on their electric bills. In hot areas like the Southwest with high air conditioning bills, solar at home can save a family thousands of dollars a year. Even in cooler, less sunny places like New York State or Massachusetts, solar has become popular because it still saves families money. Taking control of their electric bills is an important way for families to gain more financial security and autonomy.

Solar also makes households more resilient by offering them backup power in case of the kind of grid failure we talked about above. Even in the case of an ordinary blackout that only lasts a couple hours or a couple days, if solar homeowners install batteries, they can keep the lights on even if the power goes down. Today, because of high costs for batteries, most homes with solar are connected to the grid without batteries. As a result, these homes don't have the ability to get power during a power outage. When the power goes out, a home solar system also cuts off and stops sending power into the grid. This is a safety measure to protect utility workers who may be working on nearby power lines.

If you add batteries to a home solar system, then you can get around this issue. In that case, when the grid goes off, the solar system can switch over to the batteries, and keep producing power. As battery technology becomes better and cheaper, more homes will have the ability to toggle back and forth between the grid and their own batteries. At some point, homes may even forgo connecting to the grid altogether. Utility companies won't like that, because it will cost them customers and profits, but solar with storage can allow families to cut the cord from their local utility, gaining them energy independence on the home level.

If monopoly utilities keep fighting against rooftop solar, in the future, more electricity customers may just decide to leave their utility behind and go totally off grid using solar with battery storage.

From the Revolution: Sons of Liberty

In response to attempts by King George's government ministers in London in the 1760s to impose new taxes on the American colonies, Samuel Adams and other patriots in New England started the Sons of Liberty to stand up for American traditions of self-government. The group began as a semi-secret club of patriots that led boisterous street demonstrations in Boston and New York, later spreading to Virginia and the Carolinas.

To be fair, the Sons of Liberty could be rough. But they were effective. "Through the use of mob rule, tactics of fear, force, intimidation, and violence such as tar and feathering, and the stockpiling of arms, shot, and gun powder, the Sons of Liberty effectively undermined British rule, paving the way to America's independence," according to the Boston Tea Party Museum.

The Sons of Liberty later morphed into or helped inspire more respectable groups throughout the colonies, such as the Committees of Safety and the Committees of Correspondence, composed of leading citizens who helped colonies work together to coordinate boycotts and other protests against King George's new taxes. These groups matured into shadow governments for each colony that went on to take control away from royal officials in the early days of the Revolution.

Because of the revolution that the Sons of Liberty helped start in the 1770s, which ultimately gave Americans the democracy that we enjoy today, today's solar patriot does not need to resort to such rough tactics. Yet, the example of citizens across the country banding together to fight a seemingly unbeatable power and win against long odds is one that can inspire solar homeowners to stand shoulder-to-shoulder against monopoly utilities that would attack solar rights.

The Sons of Liberty can also inspire solar advocates to take up creative and powerful tactics hearkening back to the group's most famous action—the Boston Tea Party, which we'll cover in the next chapter.

Four

Why You are the Best Advocate

A good example is the best sermon.

—Benjamin Franklin

Actions speak louder than words. Many types of people advocate for solar power. These include environmentalists, solar industry representatives and employees, and local citizens. Their work is important. But unfortunately, they lack the credibility that you have as a solar homeowner. That's why they need your help!

It's a proven fact that solar spreads more quickly when neighbors can see that at least one neighbor has gone solar already. People who own solar companies already know this. That's why they tell their door-to-door salespeople to start on streets that already have at least one home with solar panels on the roof.

In his book *Rooftop Revolution*, Danny Kennedy writes that "For every one percent of new installations in an area, it was one percent faster for the next solar system to be installed in the same neighborhood," according to a study by Stanford University. Why? Both because of the power of the example of someone like you—your neighbor rather than some "crazy hippie"—and also, according to Kennedy, because the "clerk down at City Hall would be more familiar with solar installations and would process the construction permit more quickly."

An Alliance of Solar Homeowners

Anya Schoolman knows the power that solar homeowners have to stand up for solar better than almost anyone else. She's been an activist for solar power in Washington, DC since 2007.

At first, she tried getting other people who cared about clean energy to lobby for better solar incentives in the District so that it would be more affordable for homeowners to get solar. But she quickly found out that it actually worked better if she did it the other way around: Help people to go solar at home first. Then, recruit them as activists for better government rules on solar power later.

"We start with helping people go solar and then move to advocacy. What gets them excited is being able to do something concrete and practical. And they try to get engaged with the policy barriers as a side incident. It happens along the way."

With this approach, Schoolman got together with some neighbors who wanted solar to form the Mount Pleasant Coop, a purchasing club that would let them combine their solar installations into a single order to qualify for a group discount. Then, after they got solar installed, she mobilized some of those homeowners to contact the city government asking for better incentives for solar. At times, that meant arguing against the local electric utility, which wanted to slow down the progress of solar in the District of Columbia to protect the profit it was making there.

"Every step of the way we had to mobilize homeowners to go to the city council and say it's our money, ratepayer money."

By successfully lobbying for generous solar incentives and a fair electricity market for homeowners, Schoolman's group helped make the District of Columbia one of America's best places to get solar. In 2017, Solar Power Rocks ranked Washington, DC as the ninth best state or district in terms of solar incentives. To recognize her leadership on solar advocacy in the District of Columbia, in 2014 President Obama named Schoolman a "Champion of

Change," one of ten honorees who had helped bring more solar to communities around the country.

Since then, Schoolman has expanded her work with homeowners to half a dozen states. Her national umbrella organization, Solar United Neighbors, has sponsored local cooperative groups that have installed solar at a discount on more than a thousand homes, adding up to 15 megawatts of distributed solar power so far. At the same time, local affiliates in a dozen states—from SUN Alabama in Montgomery to SUN West Virginia in Charleston—have become powerful lobbying groups in their local areas, helping to pass pro-solar laws and fight government rules and regulations that would hurt solar in their state.

"We really strongly believe that people who have solar are the best people for the issue," Schoolman told me. "They care about not just solar but also the grid of the future where you have solar, storage, and an electric vehicle, and even use energy management." (Energy management is a way to plan your energy demand in advance to try to conserve energy and use it more efficiently.)

Schoolman feels that today's electric grid, which is controlled by utilities, should be more open to homeowners. Since homeowners have made a big investment in solar, then it's only fair that those same homeowners should have some say in how America's electricity system is run.

"The system should be designed so that if the homeowner is going to put their money and their energy into it then they should have a role in running it and get some of the benefit. The sharing of the financial benefit has to go with sharing the financial responsibility."

In a sense, it's symbolic equity in the electrical system, bought with their purchase of home solar, that gives solar homeowners so much authority to talk about good solar policy.

Since electric utilities often try to roll back good solar policy, Schoolman says that citizens who already have solar at home have to keep fighting. And those homeowners are the best ones to do the fighting, not only because they believe that solar is good for their community and good for America, but because they also have a financial incentive to make sure that the rules stay fair for themselves and other solar homeowners.

"It really requires an ever-growing vigilance and mobilization of people who have a vested economic interest in a different kind of market. It's just human nature, if you plunk down $15,000 for a solar energy system, then you're going to fight to protect it. A lot of people care about climate change. But there's an intensity when people have their own private property involved."

A Tale of Two States

The battles between solar supporters and electric utilities in recent years have demonstrated the power of solar homeowners. Just consider what happened in two different states when utilities came to attack net metering programs, which allow solar owners to sell their excess power back to the grid at a fair rate.

In Indiana, legislators who were friendly to utilities had been trying to repeal the state's net metering program since at least 2015, which paid solar producers for their extra solar power at the retail electricity rate. Utilities said this was too high and they wanted to reduce the rate or cancel net metering altogether. Finally, in May of 2017, after intense lobbying, those utilities got their way. That's when Indiana Governor Eric Holcomb signed a bill to shred incentives for rooftop solar. For current solar owners, it reduced net metering payments by more than 60 percent. Then, the new law ends net metering altogether for new customers after 2022. Also, in the future, utilities can make all solar homeowners pay an extra monthly fee just to stay connected to the grid.

Just as in Nevada and Florida, citizens in Indiana have overwhelmingly supported solar for years. So, it's no surprise that people in Indiana who were informed about state solar policy hated this bill when they found out how it would slow down the spread of solar in the Hoosier State. But utilities were able to get anti-solar legislation through partly because there were few homeowners with solar in the state around to lead the fight against the bill. At the time, Indiana, with a population of 6.6 million people, had only 30,000 homes powered by solar, according to the Solar Energy Industries Association.

By contrast, Nevada, a sparsely populated desert state with only half as many residents as Indiana (3 million), had a whopping 372,000 homes powered by solar in 2017. Put in terms of families, 1 in 20 Nevada households had solar but in Indiana, only 1 in 77 households had solar.

"In Indiana, you had rallies and protests. But it wasn't the same size as in Nevada, mostly because there are not many solar homeowners in Indiana," Matt Kasper of the Energy and Policy Institute explained to me. "If you talk to the Sierra Club or others who were working on this issue in Indiana, it was clever for utility companies to quickly weaken net metering in that state so you didn't have an army of solar homeowners."

Of course, with lots of sun and high electricity prices, it was natural that homeowners in Nevada would flock to solar. And over the years, the state responded by putting in good incentives, including retail net metering. It was also natural that utilities would start to feel the pinch on their profits as so many of their customers went solar and stopped buying electricity from their local utility. As a result, just as utilities did in Indiana, Nevada's utilities also tried to get the state to cut net metering payments and cancel the program, as we saw in this book's introduction.

At first, the utility lobby in Nevada was successful, as we saw. At the end of 2015, NV Energy was able to convince the state public utilities commission to cut net metering by 75 percent and triple the monthly fee for solar owners to stay connected to the grid.

"When it comes to legislators and governors, they see the utility companies as some of the top job providers in the state or the district," explained Kasper. "They provide tax revenues, they have foundations that give money to local charities. Utilities are a very large political force in any state capital. So, when they do have a meeting with a legislator, analyst, or someone at the public utility commission, they trust the utility and want to work with them as opposed to a solar group that may come from out of state."

But fortunately for solar homeowners in Nevada, despite the influence of NV Energy in Nevada's state government, the story didn't end there. In response to this decision by the state, a coalition of solar advocates began an aggressive campaign to reverse the state's anti-solar stance.

Nevada solar homeowners participated in massive demonstrations at the state capital in Carson City. Solar homeowners wrote letters, made calls, and paid visits to their state legislators. And solar homeowners appeared on TV and radio and gave interviews to newspapers. Public opinion was loud and clear in favor of a fair deal for solar homeowners.

This time, Nevada's legislators listened to the citizens instead of utilities. Pro-solar forces ultimately won the battle. In June of 2017, Governor Brian Sandoval signed Assembly bill 405 to restore net metering at nearly its previous rate and reduce the monthly charge for solar homeowners.

What made the difference in Nevada versus Indiana? In both states, the Republican Party was in control. And in both states, utilities used the influence that they had built over decades of lobbying to get a friendly ear from state officials. The big difference was the presence in Nevada of a large group of solar homeowners who stood up against the utility attack on solar.

As a result of their defeat in Nevada—and defeats around the same time to roll back rooftop solar in other states including California and Florida—utilities have learned a big lesson. They learned that they can can successfully attack the solar industry where it is weak, in states like Indiana where homeowners have just started to go solar in big numbers. But in states like Nevada with many solar homeowners who can field an army of homeowner-advocates to defend good solar regulations, then utilities can't just kill solar with impunity. Utilities know that they will face a tough fight if they want to roll back solar in states where it's well established. And in big solar states, utilities now know that trying to roll back solar in those states is a fight they will probably lose.

When it comes to spreading solar, solar homeowners are the real deal. They've already put their money where their mouth is. That makes them more credible than any other advocate for solar. If a homeowner starts with their own network—their own neighbors, family, and friends—then they can easily influence people who are already curious about solar to want to learn more. And that's the first step towards recruiting others into an army of solar champions who can stand up for rooftop solar power against attacks by electric utilities.

From the Revolution: Boston Tea Party

It would later become an inspiration to generations of Americans who wanted to protest against government support for crony capitalists. But the Boston Tea Party started as the biggest hit of the Sons of Liberty. On the night of December 6, 1773, members of the group disguised as Mohawk warriors boarded three ships in Boston Harbor and threw 342 chests of tea into the water. This lively protest was a response to the Tea Act passed by the British Parliament earlier that year, which the colonists saw as just another attempt to tax them without representation.

While a small tax was levied on tea, the real issue was that the Tea Act bolstered the monopoly of the British East India Company as the exclusive legal provider of tea to the thirteen American colonies, putting small American suppliers of tea out of business. Also, like the Stamp Act eight years earlier, the tax on tea was not introduced by the colonists themselves as was their custom, but it was imposed without consulting colonial legislatures by the British Parliament.

The Boston Tea Party led the British authorities to overreact. When news reached London in January of 1774, King George's government passed a series of laws meant to punish the colonists, known to Americans as the Intolerable Acts.

The worst of these offensive laws suspended the self-government that Massachusetts had enjoyed under its colonial charter since the days of the Pilgrims. The British also closed the busy port of Boston to all trade until the Bostonians would repay the cost of the drowned tea, destroying the livelihood of thousands of citizens of the city. Anger at this extreme response helped provoke Americans to unite across colonies in the First Continental Congress convened in Philadelphia in the fall of that year.

More than two centuries after independence, Americans have continued to take inspiration from the Tea Party's protest against British rule to stand up for their freedoms against entrenched domestic powers. Perhaps the most famous was the Tea Party movement that elected a slate of protest-minded Republicans to Congress in 2010. Today, that same movement has joined the fight for solar rights.

One of America's leading advocates for solar homeowners is Debbie Dooley, leader of the Georgia Tea Party Patriots and founder of the innovative Green Tea Coalition. Dooley became famous nationwide when she led a successful effort in 2013 to require utilities in Georgia to buy more power from solar homeowners. Later, in Florida in 2016, she helped lead the alliance of solar companies, homeowners, environmental groups, conservative activists, and others to defeat Florida's deceptive Amendment 1, which we discussed in Chapter 2.

Five

The Joy of Getting Involved

The consciousness of having discharged
that duty which we owe to our country
is superior to all other considerations.

—George Washington

It can be energizing to step outside yourself and commit to something larger. And what can be bigger than helping Americans win freedom from dirty energy, protecting the future of both our own country and the whole world?

When you start talking with people you know about solar power, you may notice that their ears perk up. Americans are a practical people who admire those who have found a better way to make money or save money.

But we're also an idealistic people who want to do our part to make life better for everybody. Few Americans quit their jobs to pursue a life dedicated only to helping others. But when we see an opportunity to make a difference while also helping ourselves, then many of us will be intrigued. That's why it's a such great idea to talk to your friends about solar.

From Small Talk to Solar Talk

Talking about something that goes beyond the usual casual conversations about sports or vacations may make you stand out a bit from the people you know. And that might take you to the edge of your comfort zone.

So, if you feel that you need permission to become a more public advocate for rooftop solar, then consider this book that permission.

But really, if you have already gone solar at home, then you don't need anyone's permission to stand up tall and proud for solar power. You've proven your commitment. And since most people do a lot of research on solar before they get their own solar panels, you probably already know more about solar power than most of your neighbors, family, and friends—and most other people in America too.

The beauty of the American system as set up by our nation's founders is that you don't need permission from anybody to get more involved. As a citizen, you are sovereign. The government works for you, not the other way around. If you feel that the government is not working well for rooftop solar these days in Washington, DC or in your state capital, then you have the right to ask for change.

The First Amendment of the United States Constitution guarantees "the right of the people…to petition the Government for a redress of grievances."

So, if you feel that utilities are using government as a tool to try to kill or slow down rooftop solar, then you have a right to demand that your government change course and start listening to citizens who want more solar power that they make themselves instead of dirty energy from monopoly utilities.

If you want to help spread solar around America, lobbying elected officials is one of the most powerful things you can do. If you're not ready for that, of course there are other things you can do to help, from just talking about solar with people you know to sending referrals to your solar installer. But I'd ask you first to simply consider how much more gratifying it might be for you to become a citizen lobbyist for solar power.

You already know how satisfying it is to get your own power from the sun, instead of having to buy it from an electric utility. Danny Kennedy, whose book *Rooftop Revolution* I mentioned earlier (and which I strongly recommend) explained to me that "Being able to tap a source of power fresh from the sky every day is the ultimate form of freedom, to be secure in what we need and not have one of those critical dependencies on gas or coal." Going solar essentially raises your status from a "dumb consumer who's just trapped in the system" to a producer of energy, one of the most important services of modern civilization.

Solar homeowners can take that liberation to the next level by becoming advocates for solar, Kennedy says. "They're citizens and the ultimate form of activism in our democracy is to fight for the right to treat your home as your castle and run it as you want. You want to get fair value for the solar power you produce. Homeowners can be the best agitators for solar to operate effectively in the market."

Yet, you might think that you can't make a difference. Maybe you think the system is so corrupt that ordinary citizens can't have much influence over politicians, who pay more attention to special interests like utility companies that make large donations to their campaigns. If you think that elected officials won't pay much attention to an ordinary solar homeowner, then you may wonder if there's any point to lobbying.

Well, just remember what happened in Nevada. There, solar homeowners made all the difference, handing a massive defeat to the powerful monopoly utility NV Energy when it attacked net metering and tried to add high discriminatory charges only for solar owners. What it took to turn back the utility's attack against good solar policies was for homeowners to get involved. And those neighbors had to be willing to work together across traditional political divides to join the same party—the rooftop solar party, that is.

Solar Unites Progressives and Conservatives

Meanwhile, in the last few years it seems that America has become divided into two nations, where conservatives and progressives can hardly agree on anything. Issues like abortion, healthcare, and taxes have always been contentious. But these days it seems that we're letting our differences of opinion in one area keep us from talking about anything else. Some historians say that the country hasn't been split this badly since the Vietnam War or even since before the Civil War. And we all know what happened back then.

Today, we may not be facing the threat of armed conflict between different regions of the country as the United States faced in 1861 or even the unrest of the 1960s. But it's a serious problem when Americans with different perspectives can't work well together to find compromises on the big problems that face the country. And one of America's biggest challenges will be to find enough clean energy to protect our economy and our way of life in the future.

Fortunately, both conservatives and progressives support rooftop solar. Solar patriots can only win the clean energy revolution against entrenched monopoly utilities and fossil fuel interests if we are willing to cooperate with citizens who may disagree with us on other issues but share a common passion for solar power.

It's natural for well-educated and well-informed citizens to disagree on what's needed to make America better. Yet, until we have a good reason to think otherwise, it's only fair to assume that we all have good motivations. In my experience, though progressives and conservatives want to take different roads to get there, we all want to reach the same destination: a country that is free and fair, prosperous and secure, offering opportunities for everyone to thrive in a natural environment with a stable climate and clean air, water, and land.

As Thomas Jefferson said, "Every difference of opinion is not a difference of principle."

You probably already know that progressives from Al Gore to the Sierra Club to the Democratic mayors of major cities like New York City, Chicago, and San Francisco are big advocates of solar power.

But you may not have heard that a growing number of conservatives and Republicans also want to see America put up more solar panels. Let's look at just a few examples here of what some conservative leaders have to say about solar power, especially when it's on your roof and it's not owned by a utility company.

Earlier, we learned how former South Carolina Congressman Bob Inglis, who we first encountered in Chapter 3, converted from climate science skeptic to climate activist.

Seeing the scientific evidence for himself was a big part of getting Inglis to change his mind. And his religious faith was a motivation for Inglis to start to do his part to protect God's creation. Ever since he became an advocate for climate solutions, Inglis has had the chance to talk to thousands of people from across the political spectrum about climate and energy. Based on this experience, Inglis told me about the different terms that progressives and conservatives—the blue and red teams—use to talk about solar.

"The blue team will talk about cleaning the air. The red team will say that solar is an opportunity for real freedom and the opportunity to turn one's roof into a productive asset and to get off the grid and to move beyond monopolistic power companies. When we get the ability to cost-effectively store that energy and put it in our cars we'll be able to say to the Middle East hey, you can drink that stuff [i.e., oil]. All those things are high-octane conservatism."

Michele Combs also lives in South Carolina, where she founded a group that has now gone nationwide, Young Conservatives for Energy Reform. She thinks that solar appeals to conservatives regardless of age. "With solar it's very appealing to conservatives because you control your energy. The government is not controlling it, but you actually control it yourself. Utility companies definitely are a monopoly," Combs told me.

Compared to many older conservatives, in her experience younger voters on the right give a higher priority to protecting the environment and fighting climate change. But the economic opportunity of solar and other clean energy is what attracts the young conservatives to Combs' organization.

"The thing that's really appealing to the young people now is jobs. Clean energy jobs are the way of the future. I live in Charleston, South Carolina, and out of 300 houses in my area, probably 50 of them have solar panels." Combs hopes to go solar at her own home soon, and a generous state tax credit in South Carolina will make it more affordable. Meanwhile, she's working to raise energy awareness among young conservatives across America.

"We have a summit every year in the fall. We bring in Republican legislators and industry leaders who talk to young leaders about going back to their states. There are great things going on all over the country that people in Washington, DC don't know about. I see it trickling up to the federal level."

As to public policy to encourage solar, Combs supports solar tax credits as well as a carbon fee to make fossil fuels pay more of their own way. Overall, she wants action at the federal level.

"I think we first have to come up with a comprehensive energy bill that will give clean energy the same amount of funding as other types of energy. We will somehow have to come up with a way to come off of fossil fuels, maybe in our children's lifetimes. We'll have to be more energy efficient and energy independent."

Mark Fleming is CEO of Conservatives for Clean Energy, based in Raleigh, North Carolina. He told me that conservatives like solar for economic reasons—jobs, energy independence, and competition. "Conservatives generally don't like big. They don't like big government. They are suspicious of a monopoly utility system. When you get the debate to that level you find a strong conservative support for anything that creates competition. The more we can help drive that conversation the better."

Ash Mason is Southeastern Regional Director at the Christian Coalition of America, a group founded in 1989 by Pat Robertson that became famous for mobilizing evangelical Christians to get involved in politics on such issues as fighting abortion. Now one of the largest grassroots organizations in the country, the Christian Coalition has added a new issue to its top five core concerns—rooftop solar.

"The Christian Coalition and Christians in general have always admired the things that make us a family," Mason told me. "Having to decide between paying the electric bill and putting food on the table are important decisions. We want to make those choices easier."

He would like to start a new mission to help churches install solar panels that can provide solar power both for the church itself and for low-income parishioners.

"Many churches move into old warehouse buildings that are perfect for solar arrays. If we can equip these churches with the ability to be energy efficient and no longer worry about a power bill then they can spend more on the ministry. Then, what if they can sell energy back into the grid? We can create a Light Credit to help those who can't afford their own power bills."

Mason is a bit of a gear-head when it comes to solar equipment. He wears a solar-powered wrist watch, and likes to talk about the latest PowerWall battery system from Tesla, as well as solar shingles and nanotechnology films that could replace crystalline solar panels in the future. Mason even earned a certificate in renewable energy management from North Carolina State University.

"I am really interested in the technology and so I feel I need to be able to explain how it works. That's why I went to seminary originally, so I can explain what I believe. I believe in giving God's honest truth and letting people make up their own mind. Hopefully that's what leaders will get back to in the future."

To learn that conservatives seem to support rooftop solar as much as progressives do is encouraging.

Bipartisan support for rooftop solar and clean energy means that there is a practical path to solve our energy and climate crisis where everybody can win. And that's good news to help solve America's political crisis. Perhaps solar could be an issue that helps bridge today's partisan divides and brings Americans with different views together around values that we all share: personal freedom, energy independence, and prosperity.

Renewable energy is already a big issue, promising benefits from climate solutions to energy independence. But solar power could also do more for America. It could help make the political climate less stormy.

Working to spread rooftop solar could bring people together across the political spectrum in a positive, cooperative way. This could help reduce the partisanship that bedevils American politics today, the very same contentiousness that George Washington himself warned against in his famous Farwell Address in 1796:

> The spirit of party...serves always to distract the Public Councils and enfeeble the Public administration. It agitates the community with ill-founded jealousies and false alarms, kindles the animosity of one part against another, foments occasionally riot and insurrection. It opens the door to foreign influence and corruption, which finds a facilitated

> access to the government itself through the channels of party passions.

Politically, solar could help unite Americans at a time when we are dangerously far apart. Future generations will surely be grateful for the work of today's solar patriots to bridge partisan divides and help people on both the left and the right to put country ahead of party.

Standing Up for Solar in a Way that Works for Your Personality

Getting involved in spreading rooftop solar around America will not only protect your investment in solar at home for the future. It could also be just what the country needs to start solving our biggest problems again.

That's a big opportunity to make a difference. But you may also think it's a bit too big. If you don't have any experience lobbying elected officials, you might wonder if you're up to it. Or maybe lobbying just isn't your thing. Either way, don't worry. There are plenty of other things besides talking to government officials that you can do to help spread solar.

You can start by just talking to your neighbors, family, and friends. Then, if you feel comfortable, you can start referring people you know who are interested in going solar to your solar installation company. Finally, once you've done some of those things, you may be ready to try your hand at a bit of citizen lobbying, by writing a letter to the editor or calling the office of your member of Congress.

So, if you're ready to get started, let's look at these options for you to get involved. We'll begin with the easy stuff and then we'll work our way up to more challenging (and rewarding) ways to stand up for solar rights. But first we'll see what lessons the American Revolution has for us on getting involved!

From the Revolution: Battles of Lexington and Concord

The first battles of the American Revolution, known as "the shots heard around the world," took place in the Massachusetts towns of Lexington and Concord on April 19, 1775. Still angry about the Tea Act and other British impositions on their local sovereignty, Americans around the colonies started to conclude that the only way to protect their rights was to throw off British rule and create an independent nation. Spurred by the Sons of Liberty, colonists in New England led the way by stockpiling arms for the day when open war would break out.

That day came when British General Thomas Gage, in his base in Boston, learned of a weapons cache held by patriots in Concord. He issued an order to his forces to march west of the city to confiscate the weapons cache in Concord and any other caches they might find in towns along the way. Patriots in Boston learned of the order, and sent Paul Revere on his legendary ride to warn the patriots of Concord and nearby towns that "the British are coming."

Forewarned was forearmed, and by the time the column of 700 British soldiers reached Lexington on April 19, seventy Minutemen were waiting for them. After a tense standoff on Lexington Green between local patriots and the far larger British force, a shot was fired by an unknown gun, and widespread shooting began. A similar scene was repeated later that day when the British reached nearby Concord.

More than a year later and after more armed engagements including the Battle of Bunker Hill outside of Boston, the colonists would formally break with the British crown and declare their independence.

For today's solar patriots, attacks on net metering by Arizona utilities were the Lexington and Concord of the battle to protect solar rights, according to Court Rich, an attorney involved in solar policy.

"In the early battles, you learn about your opponents and their strategies," Rich told a solar industry conference in 2017. The nationwide fight over net metering began in Arizona.

In 2013, the Arizona Corporation Commission became the first regulatory body in a major solar market to allow a utility (Arizona Public Service) to impose a discriminatory charge on solar system owners. Utilities took these attacks from Arizona into other states including Nevada and Florida, as we've seen. But solar patriots in those states fought back—and like our scrappy forefathers, they won!

Six

Education—Help Create More Demand for Solar

It does not take a majority to prevail but rather an irate, tireless minority, keen on setting brushfires of freedom in the minds of men.

—Samuel Adams

If you think that education only happens in school and that only teachers are the ones who educate people, you should think again. Education happens anytime a person, whether a child or an adult, learns something new.

The Founding Fathers thought that an educated citizenry was necessary for a republican system of government to work in America or anywhere else.

For example, in 1816 Thomas Jefferson wrote to a friend, "If a nation expects to be ignorant and free in a state of civilization, it expects what never was and never will be. If we are to guard against ignorance and remain free, it is the responsibility of every American to be informed."

To use another example, James Madison said that "Knowledge will forever govern ignorance; and a people who mean to be their own governors must arm themselves with the power which knowledge gives."

Because they knew that government by the people would only work if the people were well informed, early American leaders supported freedom of the press. And they went even further than that, getting involved with the media themselves as a way to educate the public. Franklin, Jefferson, Madison, and Hamilton all had their hands in newspapers, whether printing and publishing them, writing articles for them or having others do so on their behalf. When he was president, Jefferson made sure that new territories out west included a funding source to set up local public schools.

Americans already overwhelmingly support solar power and want the economy to use more of it, according to numerous surveys. But Americans usually don't know much about solar power. As a result, most people may think that solar is becoming one of our country's top energy sources already and that it doesn't need any help. Ordinary citizens may also think that utilities are putting in enough large solar plants on their own that homeowners don't need to install solar on their own roofs.

One of the most important things that you can do to help spread solar power around America is to start educating people you know about energy. You don't need to stand at the front of a classroom or a lecture hall to do it. It will be most effective, and come most naturally, if you just talk to people casually about energy and about solar power through your ordinary encounters with them as you go through your daily routine or at relaxed social events.

What Qualifies You to Educate People on Solar

Are you qualified to educate people about energy? Absolutely.

First, as we've seen, if you've already gone solar yourself, then people who know you will think of you as an authority. And they should see you as an authority. By paying to have solar panels installed on your home, you've certainly put your money where your mouth is on solar.

Second, I'm sure that before you got solar panels, you did some research on your own about solar and about your options to go solar. You probably learned how photovoltaic technology converts light into electric power. You may also have learned about equipment such as modules, inverters, and racking. You probably also learned about advancements in technology that make solar power more efficient and more affordable today.

You certainly got into the economics of solar, especially how many kilowatts of solar capacity you needed to get to cover your home's electricity demand. You also had to learn about financing, whether you should buy your solar system in cash up front, get a loan, lease the panels or just get the electricity through a power purchase agreement. And you probably learned how soon your solar panels would pay for themselves, after which you'd have essentially free energy.

After your journey to go solar, these and other topics relating to electricity and energy may now be familiar to you. But don't assume that other people are as comfortable talking about solar power or electricity as you are. The good news is that Americans are interested in solar. The bad news is that most people don't know much about solar power in particular or about energy in general. And some of the things they think they do know about energy are wrong.

Don't Know Nothin' about Energy

Drivers can tell you the cost of a gallon of gas at the local station on any given day. And most people who pay their bills for their home, apartment, or small business have been heard to complain from time to time that energy companies make too much profit off the backs of ordinary Americans. As to electricity, most people know how to turn on a light switch, turn down a thermostat—and of course, complain about the power company. And that's about all they know about energy.

Given how important energy is to modern life, Americans' energy literacy is shockingly low. And the biggest problem is that most people aren't aware of how little they actually know about energy. Nine out of ten Americans think they know about energy, and one in three thinks they know a lot about energy, according to a recent study. Yet, when you ask people where their energy comes from, well, their guesses are a bit off.

"Americans seriously overestimate how much electricity we get from renewables," says a 2016 survey of more than a thousand ordinary consumers from a company called Makovsky that advises the energy industry on communications.[10]

When it comes to solar power, the two most interesting numbers are:

- Americans think that the country today gets 11 percent of its electricity from solar power. The truth is, despite rapid growth in the last few years, American's still only get about 1 percent of our total electricity from solar.

- Likewise, Americans think that in five years solar will provide 20 percent of America's electricity. But the U.S. Energy Information Administration predicts that solar will still only produce just over 1 percent of the nation's power. (Note: The EIA's estimate is conservative. Other experts may predict higher numbers for solar power in the next five years, but none of them are even close to 20 percent).

It's safe to say today that Americans do think that the country uses more solar than we actually do. Much more.

Is that a problem? Only if it makes Americans complacent about pushing for more solar.

If citizens think that we have enough solar already, that we'll get plenty more in the future by just letting things go on as they have been, and that grid electricity is basically pretty clean, then they won't see much urgency to demand more solar, especially on rooftops of homes and small businesses.

If they're too optimistic about the ability of electric utilities to provide them solar power if they simply check a box on their electric bill to join their local utility's "green power" program, then ordinary citizens won't worry about whether America is moving in the right direction on solar or not.

In that case, citizens may not bother to demand that utilities start offering more solar to their ratepayers.

Citizens also won't demand that utilities stop trying to prevent homeowners from getting their own solar. And if they think the electric company has got the issue of solar power covered, then families won't bother to make the investment in getting their own solar panels at home.

Solar has accomplished a lot so far just to get to one percent of America's power supply. But obviously, there's plenty of room for growth. You can help make that growth happen sooner rather than later by educating people you know about the role of solar in our economy today and how much potential there is for solar to grow in the near future. Too many people believe outdated ideas or myths about solar that prevent them from taking solar seriously.

For example, while many Americans think that the electricity they buy from their utility has much more solar power than it actually does, other people think the opposite—that there's not much solar today and that there never will be.

That's because, in the minds of these people, solar power is still an "experimental" energy source that requires more "research" to become practical. That might have been true in the 1970s. But it's not true anymore. As solar homeowners can attest from their own experience, solar panels are ready to go up on your roof today. Solar is ready to start producing clean energy at your home right away.

You, as a solar homeowner, are uniquely qualified to bust myths about solar and help spread the truth to the people you know.

In Appendix A at the end of this book is a list of other common myths about solar power along with a short response to each myth that gives the truth. You can use this list in conversations with your friends, family, and neighbors. Or, you can even give your own presentations about solar power.

Become A Local Solar Expert

If you're ready to step up and do more, you can become a recognized solar expert in your local area.

As someone with solar panels, local clubs and groups that you belong to will recognize that you are qualified to talk about solar power from your knowledge and personal experience. And because solar power is such a hot topic these days, local groups know that their members would probably like to hear more about solar. So, if you approach a group that regularly hosts speakers on topics of current interest, and if you're already a member of that group, then if you offer to talk about solar power based on your experience as a solar homeowner, you'll probably get some interest.

Some solar homeowners give talks at local meetings such as those held by homeowners and neighborhood associations, church groups, or a chapter of the Rotary Club. You can even organize your own talk at a nearby public library or offer yourself as a speaker at your kids' school.

Just as it is with educating people you know through conversations about solar, public speaking is not as scary as you might think.

There are ways to make it easier to give a public talk. Some of the groups listed at the end of this book offer free training to help you make effective presentations. If you're an outgoing person, speaking to groups can be fun—and it can help you influence people, maybe even in ways you never expected.

As Ben Franklin wrote, "Hide not your talents. They for use were made. What's a sundial in the shade?" And whether you influence anyone or not, you'll feel stronger and more alive after you give a talk. And you probably *will* influence people, perhaps in ways you hadn't expected.

Because you'll be talking to people who are presumably interested in solar already, you can have a big impact. These are people who are ready for your message and are just looking for some help—and an example from someone like them—to learn more about solar themselves.

From the Revolution: Thomas Paine's "Common Sense"

At a time when many Americans still wanted to reconcile with the British Crown, Thomas Paine argued that after so many attacks on colonists' rights by the British authorities, efforts by colonists to appease George III were against "common sense." While other writers in the colonies believed that King George III would soon rectify the wrongs done to the colonies, in his pamphlet *Common Sense,* Paine wrote that the entire British system was rotten to the core because it was based on a tyranny of aristocracy and monarchy that could never allow for true freedom.

Paine urged colonies to sever their ties to England once and for all and then to set up their own democratic government with a written constitution guaranteeing rule by the people instead of by kings and aristocrats. Leaving the British imperial system would allow Americans to enjoy the benefits of free trade with other nations besides Britain and prevent Americans from being constantly dragged into Britain's frequent European wars.

"Everything that is right or reasonable pleads for separation. The blood of the slain, the weeping voice of nature cries 'Tis time to part'," wrote Paine.

Though it was only a pamphlet of 47 pages, *Common Sense* became the best-selling book of the 18th century in North America, selling 120,000 copies in the weeks after it came out on January 19, 1776. Its ideas were not new, but *Common Sense* was the first publication to put the idea in print that colonists should declare their independence from Britain. And Paine wrote in clear, simple prose that ordinary Americans could understand, gaining him a wide readership.

As a result, the pamphlet strengthened the resolve of those who wanted independence while helping recruit new supporters to the cause. Less than six months after Paine published *Common Sense*, on July 4, delegates of all the colonies gathered in Philadelphia to ratify the Declaration of Independence.

Later that same year, in December of 1776, Paine published a second pamphlet called *The American Crisis*. While his first pamphlet helped push Americans over the edge into declaring independence, this second booklet may have helped save the revolution once it had begun. The second pamphlet's famous words still have a powerful ring today: "These are the times that try men's souls: The summer soldier and the sunshine patriot will, in this crisis, shrink from the service of their country; but he that stands it now, deserves the love and thanks of man and woman. Tyranny, like Hell, is not easily conquered; yet we have this consolation with us, that the harder the conflict, the more glorious the triumph."

Getting copies hot off the press, Washington had *The American Crisis* read aloud to his troops before crossing the Delaware River to attack Trenton, New Jersey, which we'll discuss in Chapter 9. The inspiration that Paine provided helped give the Americans the motivation to take a big risk in facing a formidable foe and, ultimately, triumph both at Trenton and in their whole long war for independence from Britain.

For today's solar patriot, Paine's little pamphlets with the big impact show the power of education to change minds and mobilize citizens for action.

Seven

Referrals—Help Others to Go Solar at Home

It takes time to persuade men to do even what is for their own good.

—Thomas Jefferson

To start with a more recent quote, Ronald Reagan said that "All great change in America begins at the dinner table."The easiest way to help spread solar is to encourage your neighbors and your family and friends to go solar at their own homes. It may also be the most rewarding for you—financially.

As we saw earlier, research shows that solar spreads more quickly once there's at least one solar installation in a neighborhood. Joining a solar installer's referral program can be an effective way for you to help spread solar power quickly to rooftops in your neighborhood and beyond.

Solar Companies Love Referrals

Referrals are valuable sales leads for solar companies. For some solar installers, referrals from existing customers are their top source of new business. Below you'll find some examples of referral programs from solar installers around the country, with details accurate as of mid-2017. If you are interested in sending referrals to any of the companies mentioned or any other solar installer, you should check with the company for current information about their referral programs.

Baker Electric Solar in San Diego gets 63 percent of their new customers from referrals. Aside from having lots of glowing reviews from satisfied customers online, Baker Electric may also get lots of referrals because they don't just sit around hoping that their customers will send people to the company and then wait for the referrals to come in. Instead, Baker Electric has established an active customer referral program.

The program starts by offering advice and encouragement for customers to talk to their friends about solar power. "If you've experienced the benefits of solar, don't keep them to yourself!" the company's referral webpage says.

> Share with your friends the many benefits of going solar. Tell them about the money and headaches you've saved by becoming your own energy provider. Let them know how it feels to take control of your energy needs and secure a lifestyle for your family that's independent from utility companies. Describe your experience with our consultants, engineers, and technicians; our 10-step installation process; and our customer service. And by all means, please convey the important fact that by switching to solar, you're doing your part to help eliminate harmful greenhouse gases in your community.

Then, Baker Electric offers a referral bonus. Payments to existing customers who send referrals to the company that sign up for solar range from a few hundred dollars for the first referral to a maximum of a thousand dollars for subsequent referrals.

Throw a Solar Party, Earn Referral Fees

Many solar installation companies offer a bonus for referrals. The amount of the bonus typically ranges from $200 to $700, though it can be as high as $1,500 or even more.

Most referral programs only make bonus payments when a potential customer who was referred by someone else signs up for solar with the company. But Clean Solar in Northern California goes further to encourage people to send them referrals. When a referral signs up for a free solar quote, the company gives the person who sent the referral a $25 gift. After that, they pay $500 for a closed deal.

To help you help them, most solar companies can offer you brochures and other printed sales materials. Companies can even consult with you on the best ways to talk about solar to prospective buyers.

For example, Northeast Solar in Massachusetts offers an attractively designed fact sheet that their customers can give out to folks they know who are interested in going solar. The fact sheet does much of the talking, with brief but helpful information on how solar can save homeowners money, how it helps the environment, how long solar panels last, and what warranties are available in case something needs to be fixed.

Some solar installation companies will even help you throw an event to introduce your friends and family to solar power.

For example, SunCraft Solar, also located in San Diego, will create a customized email text for a customer to send out to potential referrals. The email can serve as a stand-alone sales message or it can be an invitation to an event to learn more about solar power and hear the company's sales pitch. Then, SunCraft can help you set up and hold the event, whether at your home, your workplace, or even your church.

And SunCraft doesn't just send a rep to speak to the group about the benefits of solar, as many solar companies will. This company goes above and beyond by helping you throw your party in style: they provide wine and cheese for a house party or even hot dogs and soda for a neighborhood BBQ.

It will be easiest and most effective for you to refer people to the company that installed your solar panels if you are happy with their work and if they offer a referral program. In case your solar company doesn't offer a referral program, other solar installers in your area may. These can include both local installers and large national companies.

Once you get solar yourself, it's fun to show it off to your neighbors and other people you know. Earning referral payments from a solar company is a nice bonus. But the biggest satisfaction may be helping other people to do what you've already done and helping give them clean energy independence while spreading solar around your area. The story of one homeowner with solar will illustrate this well.

Case Study: The Easy Way to Get Neighbors into Solar

Paul Triolo lives in the Maryland suburbs of Washington, DC, where he commutes to his job as a consultant on international cybersecurity. In early 2017, Paul and his wife signed up for a solar cooperative program in Montgomery County which gave them a 15 percent discount on a solar installation.

The solar coop was run by SUN Maryland, an organization founded by Anya Schoolman, the solar activist with Solar United Neighbors based in Washington, DC who we met in Chapter 3. The Maryland group helped put local homeowners together to qualify for a group discount on solar installations.

"A retired couple went solar first and they were an inspiration for us," Paul told me. "Our street now has four solar installations on the block, and in our neighborhood, there are half a dozen, compared to none a couple years ago. The concept of the consortium is catching on, when you can cut the cost. It seems like a good model."

The consortium got its price break because its members all agreed to get solar from the same local company, Solar Energy World. As a result, the company installed a total of 8.6 kilowatts of solar panels on the roof of the house that Paul and his wife own. The company even paid a referral bonus to another couple who had referred the Triolos a couple years earlier.

The Triolos' solar system was designed to offset 90 percent of the couple's electricity usage over the course of a year. They plan to have Tesla PowerWall batteries installed in the future, when the price comes down, so that they don't have to use any dirty electricity from the grid.

"I still have a problem burning any carbon. I'd rather just be full electric. That's why solar is the best solution all the way round," Paul told me.

In the meantime, their Chevy Bolt electric car acts as a mobile battery backup for their solar panels.

Just as the installer, Solar Energy World, paid the other couple when the Triolos went solar, so now the company pays the Triolos $500 for their own signed referrals. Even before their solar system was a month old, Paul and his wife started spreading the word to neighbors and friends. As a result, they quickly earned one referral commission payment and had another two couples lined up who would probably go solar as well.

They also planned to host an open house to show off their solar panels and their electric car and talk about energy efficiency upgrades that had helped make their place essentially a zero-energy house.

Paul put a lot of thought and planning into his investments in solar power and energy independence, so he enjoys sharing them with people he knows. He likes being a leader in clean technology and he enjoys pioneering new technology. That's why he might not wait until batteries are much cheaper before he installs his own energy storage system at home.

"You make your decision to buy based on the whole package, the future of the planet, what kind of system you're leaving for whoever buys the house."

From the Revolution: Continental Army

The American farmers who fought at Lexington and Concord and other early battles of the Revolution were not an organized army. Instead, they were recruits from local militia companies, groups of citizens who trained in their free time to defend their villages and farms from attacks by Native Americans. After the local militias fought the British at Lexington and Concord, they joined other militia units from around New England to lay siege to the British garrison in Boston.

At that time, the Second Continental Congress meeting in Philadelphia was still a year away from declaring independence. Some state representatives still wanted to make peace with Britain. But with more than 17,000 militiamen besieging British-occupied Boston, Congress realized that, whether they wanted it or not, they now had an army on their hands that was already fighting the British.

At the request of delegates from New England, on June 14, 1775, Congress adopted the militia units besieging Boston, designating them the Continental Army. On the next day, Congress unanimously voted to appoint George Washington to command the new American army.

Much like the state militias of Massachusetts, Connecticut, Rhode Island, and New Hampshire that formed the core of Washington's young army, today's homeowners fighting for solar rights are usually found working with groups in their own states, from California and Nevada to Florida and New York. And just as during the American Revolution, militia units became stronger when they united with those from other states in the Continental Army, so today, solar homeowners can become much more effective if they unite across states and across party lines.

A modern-day, peaceful Continental Army of solar patriots could go beyond standing up for net metering or against fixed charges in their own state. Such a national alliance of solar patriots could push for much more powerful policies on the national level.

Solar advocacy groups including Vote Solar, Solar United Neighbors, and others listed in Appendix D, bring together solar advocates across states to exchange ideas and share resources to make lobbying in separate states more effective. In a broader approach, Citizens' Climate Lobby leapfrogs past state policy altogether to push for carbon-fee-and-dividend at the federal level, the "killer app" for solar discussed later, in Chapter 10.

Thanks to the rights that the Continental Army won for Americans by force of arms nearly two and a half centuries ago, today's continent-wide army of solar patriots can fight for solar rights using peaceful means. While Washington's army defeated the superior British forces with muskets and rifles, swords and bayonets, and well-placed artillery pieces, so today's army of solar patriots can defeat the powerful forces of monopoly utilities and coal and oil barons with the peaceful weapons of education, referrals, and advocacy.

Eight

Advocacy—Support Better Public Policy for Solar

Those who expect to reap the blessings of freedom must, like men, undergo the fatigue of supporting it.

—Thomas Paine

Now we come to the part of this book that's most oriented towards the government.

In the last couple of chapters, we talked about ways that solar homeowners could help spread solar by talking to their friends, family, neighbors, and others they already know. Here, we're going to talk about how to talk to public officials about rooftop solar.

It's not actually as hard as you might think to approach and make contact with government officials, especially your representatives in Congress and in your state legislature. But to do it right, you'll want to be a bit more organized than when talking with your friends. That will take some planning.

So, to decide if it's worthwhile for you to make the effort, let's start by talking about why the government matters when it comes to spreading solar power.

Why Solar Needs the Government on Its Side

Some people think that the government has no place in helping more Americans to go solar. Homeowners who want to go solar can just do it on their own, right?

They can buy solar panels, get financing to make it affordable, and then sit back and enjoy their clean energy for years to come. This seems like something that could happen entirely within the consumer marketplace, as a transaction between a homeowner and a solar installer. The only other thing that you need is a little cooperation from the local utility company that needs to give permission to hook the solar system up to the electric grid.

Of course, anyone who's gone solar at home already knows that it's not so simple. Buying solar panels is not a simple consumer transaction for a home improvement like paving your driveway or replacing your gutters.

The main difference with solar is that the government *is already* involved in several different ways. Some of those ways are helpful, making solar cheaper and easier to get and more effective to run once you get it. But sometimes government, especially when it's listening to utility companies, actually does things to slow down the spread of solar.

Let's talk a little bit about how the government, at both the state and federal level, can help or hurt rooftop solar power.

Energy Subsidies

Anyone who's gotten solar power at home knows that government subsidies can cut the price of a solar system by 50 percent or even more. The main subsidy available across the country is the 30 percent Solar Federal Investment Tax Credit, currently scheduled to remain at full force through 2019, after which time it will decline in value and then disappear entirely for homeowners after 2021.

In addition, depending on where you live, many states also offer subsidies for homeowners who go solar. States usually offer two types of incentives. First, states offer incentives to cut the initial price of a solar installation such as tax credits and exemptions along with direct cash grants and low-interest loans. Second, once a solar system is installed, states may offer other incentives to make solar cheaper to own over the long term such as net energy metering, where solar owners can sell their excess power back to the electric grid at a fair rate, usually the same rate per kilowatt hour that they pay their electric company for power.

Are Solar Incentives Fair?

Is it fair that solar power receives these incentives? And are they necessary for solar to spread?

Critics say that giving incentives to homeowners to get solar is a waste of taxpayer money.

"Solar energy can't survive without massive subsidies," according to Benjamin Zycher of the American Enterprise Institute.[11] Without incentives, solar would actually be very expensive, this argument goes.

That's because, so critics claim, solar is not a competitive energy source and America gains little economic benefit from promoting more solar. So, the government should stop subsidizing solar and other clean energy and instead, Americans should let the free market figure out through supply and demand the right price for solar. The government should not "pick winners" among sources of energy, which just distorts the energy marketplace. "The time has come to allow market forces to work," Zycher writes.

The thinking here is that without incentives, solar will be so expensive that almost nobody will buy it. Americans who want the lowest-cost electricity will just let their utility choose the cheapest sources of energy. Presumably, critics like Zycher say, as long as solar doesn't get unfair subsidies that make it artificially cheap compared to conventional energy sources, for years to come utilities will continue to use fossil fuels and nuclear power because they're naturally the cheapest.

Well, even if that were true, it sounds like a terrible idea.

Abandoning solar would be a disaster both for the environment and for America's economy in the long run. The Chinese and other leading solar nations will keep installing more solar panels whether America does it or not. In 2015 China became the world's largest producer of photovoltaic power, with 43 gigawatts of total installed capacity. From 2005 to 2014, production of solar cells in China expanded 100-fold. And as the world's manufacturing powerhouse, China will keep making cheaper and better solar panels to sell to the rest of the world even if America's solar manufacturers are forced to close up shop.

More importantly, how much solar depends on subsidies now and whether solar power will need subsidies in the near future to compete against other energy sources is a matter of debate.

Since prices came down 80 percent on solar panels for home use between 2008 and 2013 according to the GW Solar Institute, and have continued to drop rapidly since then, the United States may now be reaching the point where solar can compete on price against traditional electricity sources even without financial assistance from the government.[12]

This is already the case in states with high electricity prices like Hawaii. In the next five or ten years, as the price of solar continues to decline, solar will be the cheapest source of electricity in more and more parts of the country, starting with California and northeastern states that also have high electricity costs. Ultimately, solar will become so cheap that it will expand into areas like the Southeast that have some of the lowest utility rates in the nation.

Just think about it. If Thomas Paine were around today, he'd call it *common sense*.

That is, common sense tells you that if you have two sources of energy, where one source of energy requires you to keep purchasing fuel (coal, gas, or uranium for nuclear power) and the other source of energy has a fuel that's free of charge (sunlight), then the one with the free fuel will be cheaper, right?

All you need to make it happen is to get the equipment in place. And to get over that initial barrier of constructing solar arrays across the nation is why solar still needs help from government in the form of incentives.

All Energy Sources Get Subsidies

What people who criticize subsidies for solar power often fail to mention is that all major energy sources in America get government subsidies. That includes coal, oil, natural gas, and nuclear power but also less proven—or even disproven—sources of energy like corn ethanol.

In fact, subsidies for fossil fuels and nuclear power are much higher than those for solar, even when you just consider the direct financial subsidies. Over the period of time they've been subsidized, fossil fuels and nuclear power have gotten many times more subsidies over time than solar has, according to a 2011 study by DBL Investors.[13]

When you average subsidies out over the period that these energy sources have been subsidized, all renewable energy (including solar with wind and others) has cost taxpayers about $395 million per year. By contrast, nuclear power, subsidized for a much longer period, has averaged $3.57 billion annually. But the winner by far for government subsidies is oil and gas, getting an average of $4.91 billion in government subsidies *per year.*

This means that the oil and gas industry alone gets more than ten times the government subsidies given to solar and all other renewable energy combined. That's a lot of money to support a mature industry that probably hasn't needed help in about a century. That's also a lot of money to give to dirty energy that pumps out greenhouse gases and makes climate change—and human health—worse.

Taxpayer subsidies to oil and gas serve as a way to encourage Americans to use more dirty energy. And why exactly do we want to do that?

"But wait," as they say on infomercials, "there's more!"

Not only do fossil fuels and nuclear power get direct subsidies including cash payments, tax credits, low interest loans, and subsidized insurance all paid for by taxpayers. But dirty energy companies also get lots of other freebies that American taxpayers have to pay for, whether they know it or not.

If you consider indirect subsidies that make it possible for American consumers to get traditional energy in the first place, then the level of subsidy for fossil fuels and nuclear power goes way up. These include the cost for the U.S. Navy to keep open shipping lanes for oil tankers in the Persian Gulf or decades of federal research on nuclear fission. Then, to be fair, you should add in the cost of pollution from traditional energy, from healthcare bills for kids with asthma who breathe in coal dust to the cost of buying bottled water in communities where water sources have been tainted by chemicals from fracking for natural gas.

Add all those costs up—especially costs from pollution and health impacts[14] combined with costs for the military[15]—and a gallon of gasoline could go for $20 a gallon or more. Meanwhile, if you add in costs from pollution, electricity from coal or natural gas could cost much more than the current national average of 12 cents a kilowatt hour.[16]

So, people who complain about energy subsidies should look at the whole picture. And when they do, they'll see that subsidies for solar are small potatoes compared to subsidies for traditional energy. The prize for corporate welfare in America must surely go to fossil fuel and nuclear power companies, the biggest crony capitalists since the days of the Robber Barons in the nineteenth century when railroads and mining companies acquired land out west from the federal government at pennies an acre.

All this is to say that it's the American Way to subsidize energy sources. We do it because we know that affordable energy is crucial to our economy.

In the future, it might be fair to get rid of all energy subsidies, both those for new energy sources like solar and wind but also those for fossil fuels and nuclear power. There are good ideas to do that circulating in political circles today. If you decide to get involved in advocacy, you might want to support one of those proposals.

But until solar is better established and until subsidies for traditional energy are cut, it would be unfair to slash incentives for solar. In fact, government subsidies should probably be increased *and* extended at least for the next few years while the solar industry continues to mature.

Protecting Utilities from Competition by Rooftop Solar

So, as solar has grown up from a new energy source, government support for solar has been important. As it continues to supply more of America's electricity, and economies of scale help make solar more affordable, solar power won't need as much help from the government to succeed. But what solar still needs and will always need is a level playing field with fossil fuels and nuclear power.

That means the government shouldn't help traditional energy sources more than it helps solar. If anything, government should discourage dirty energy and encourage clean energy to meet America's goals for clean air and water, to help promote a healthier populace, and to help fight climate change. Fair energy policy also means that the government should not do anything to oppose solar or impede its progress.

Unfortunately, the government, both in Washington and in state capitals across the country, continues to offer more help to already successful and prosperous traditional energy companies than it offers to solar. And even worse, in many cases the government puts up barriers to solar that make it more difficult for families who want solar to afford it.

Why? The reason is clear. State and federal government rules that make solar more expensive or harder to get don't offer any public benefit. Such roadblocks to solar merely act to protect the profits of monopoly electric utilities.

That's why some states make it hard for homeowners to sell their power back to the grid through net metering or to buy solar power from a shared solar array that's not located on their own property by outlawing "community solar" programs.

In response to ratepayer demand or state government mandates, some utilities have reluctantly started to install their own solar generation. Other utilities have started to see the benefits to solar for themselves. In either case, whether utilities want to go solar or if they are forced to go solar, the general approach of utilities to solar power has been to try to keep most of it to themselves, rather than let homeowners do it.

By now, most utilities know that solar is coming and that there's nothing they can do to stop it. So, you might think that utilities would decide that if you can't beat 'em, then you should join 'em. And in a perverse way, that is actually what most utilities are planning these days. They want to transition into solar. But they're usually not interested in getting solar from more homeowners and small businesses. Instead, utilities' idea of joining the solar revolution is to own the solar arrays themselves and lock out small solar producers. In that way, utilities can maintain their lucrative government-subsidized monopoly over America's electrical power for decades to come.

To provide America more clean energy capacity, any solar is good solar. It's certainly a good thing if utilities install big solar arrays that they can plug into the grid to supply their customers with clean energy. But in order to have a resilient electricity system that can withstand attacks by hackers or terrorists on the one hand or good old fashioned natural disasters on the other hand, centralized generation using solar is not good enough. America also needs distributed solar on rooftops across the country.

Besides, making your own clean energy at home is the right of every American homeowner. Monopoly special interests that try to stop a homeowner from fortifying their castle with solar panels are acting like tyrants who seek to deprive ordinary citizens of their property rights.

To protect our rights to go solar affordably at home and in our small businesses, Americans must stand up for those rights. That's what solar homeowners did in Nevada in 2016 and 2017, when they beat back the lobbying campaign by the monopoly utility NV Energy to destroy net metering and add high fixed monthly charges that discriminated against solar homeowners. That's also what solar supporters did in Florida in the fall of 2016 when they defeated the utilities' deceptive anti-solar ballot initiative, Amendment 1. Now, anyone who wants more solar must continue to stand up for solar rights in statehouses across the country and in Washington, DC too.

There are many good ideas for public policy that would help spread solar.

For example, the Solar Energy Industries Association offers some good ideas. These include allowing different households to share a single solar array (community solar), making it easier to get permits from local governments and to get a new solar installation connected to the grid, and treating solar owners fairly in terms of payments for electricity, utility rate structures, and even access to the grid. You can find a list of SEIA's recommended policies for rooftop solar in Appendix C at the end of this book.

Changing Public Policy

So, now that you see how important it is that state and federal governments change laws and rules to encourage solar while taking away laws and regulations that slow solar down, what can you do about it?

The way to change laws in our system is to "petition the government for a redress of grievances," as it says in the Constitution. And that means lobbying.

You may not see yourself as a lobbyist. But while there are certainly slick professionals in Washington, DC or in your state capital who fit the stereotype of an attorney in Armani suits handsomely paid by moneyed special interests to work their Rolodex of contacts from the golf course to get VIP access to legislators and their staffs, most people who lobby public officials are actually ordinary citizens.

Pamela Cargill works in the solar industry, and she had never seen herself as a lobbyist until she became one. As a management consultant based in the San Francisco Bay Area, Cargill advises solar installers on how to improve their business. That never involved much contact with government officials until Cargill joined a group from the Solar Energy Industries Association in early 2017 to fly to Washington, DC and meet with new Energy Secretary Rick Perry.

Perry was considering reducing funding for national laboratories that provided research helpful to the solar industry. Also, the department's SunShot Initiative had helped make solar more affordable. Cargill's group was there to make the case for SunShot and to keep the labs open and fully funded.

"We were able to tell some compelling stories of how research from the national labs have been commercialized by some of the companies sitting in the room and how SunShot helped those companies," Cargill told me. "These were concrete examples of how the Department of Energy is helping make solar more cost competitive and reliable."

Cargill told me how her group of solar industry executives needed to find common ground with Perry, who understood the value of wind power from his time as governor of Texas but knew little about solar power. The group tried to help Perry make that connection and see the value of federal programs to help spread solar power.

As of mid-2017, the SunShot program and the national labs have escaped the worst budget cuts.

Lobbying also worked in Nevada's net metering fight in 2016. There, solar industry professionals were joined by solar homeowners who showed up to public meetings, demonstrated in front of government offices, and called the offices of public officials. And working together with allies from other groups, solar homeowners were successful in saving Nevada's solar industry.

Citizen activism is a model that's worked in fights with utilities over solar in other states, from California to New York. And it will work again in future fights with utilities over solar rights. Indeed, according to experts on government, citizen lobbying is one of the most powerful ways to make change in our society.

"People writing letters, sending emails, attending town hall meetings, visiting lawmakers—they are the dominant influence in legislative outcomes," writes Congressional expert Bradford Fitch in his *Citizen's Handbook to Influencing Elected Officials*. In writing this informative book, Fitch got unusually close access to members of Congress from both parties. His research showed that, contrary to what you may see on TV, citizens have much more power to get laws changed than special interests do. And that's according to members of Congress themselves. Just take one example from hundreds of interviews that Fitch conducted on Capitol Hill:

> "I prioritize everything based on anything that's connected to constituents," said one Republican lawmaker. "I want feedback from the real world," he said.

Likewise, activists who are experienced in lobbying elected officials say the same thing.

"The old adage that politics is local rings true," Tyson Grinstead, the policy director covering the Southeastern U.S. for the national solar installation company Sunrun told me. "Each state has its own local way of phrasing things, so when you have a letter to the editor from someone who's passionate about solar in the community that a legislator recognizes, it means so much more than a phone call from a lobbyist or someone that legislator has met once or twice."

Grinstead thinks that it's not just helpful for solar homeowners to contact government officials about solar—it's essential for real progress. As Grinstead explains,

> Utilities have had great practice working within the political system. Lately, we've seen that citizens who are willing to participate can change the outcome of a political fight. It's helped anywhere we've had a campaign, where we've had substantial support from the public. People are asking for choice, to be fairly compensated for the energy they send back to the grid. Those folks are changing the outcomes of those policy battles and helping us to advocate effectively.

To take another example, the bipartisan group Citizens' Climate Lobby has successfully helped to recruit dozens of members of Congress, both Republicans and Democrats, as supporters of solutions to fight climate change. The group's goal is to create "political will for a livable world" and here's how they do it:

> Politicians don't create political will, they respond to it. We believe citizens who are well-trained, organized, and with a good system of support can more than influence the political process. We invite

> you to live into the opportunity that democracy offers, and in exercising that right as citizens, lift your nation to the task at hand on global warming and climate change, that of protecting our ability to live on planet Earth.

Whether your issue is climate change, energy independence, or personal empowerment, lobbying for solar is all about accepting the invitation that our democratic republic offers to stand up for what you believe in.

From the Revolution: Declaration of Independence

As we've seen, after the British imposed restrictions on trade and immigration, started quartering soldiers in civilian homes, and imposed new taxes from afar, patriot groups expanded across the colonies to coordinate protests against the increasingly heavy hand of British rule. After the British showed that they wouldn't tolerate colonists stockpiling weapons by attacking Lexington and Concord, local patriot groups ousted royal governors in each colony and took control over governments of the new states.

By the spring of 1776, enough colonists were clamoring for independence that the Second Continental Congress was ready to consider the resolution of Richard Henry Lee, delegate of Virginia, "That these united Colonies are, and of right ought to be, free and independent states." Congress appointed a committee including John Adams, Benjamin Franklin, and Thomas Jefferson to flesh out the details of the resolution in writing. After long debate, many edits, and a tense vote, Congress voted for independence on July 4, though the declaration document did not gain all its signatures until August 2.

"When in the course of events, it becomes necessary for one people to dissolve the political bands which have connected them with another, and to assume among the powers of the earth, the separate and equal station to which the laws of nature and of nature's God entitle them, a decent respect to the opinions of mankind requires that they should declare the causes which impel them to the separation."

So begins one of the most important documents in history and the founding charter of the United States, which goes on to declare that "all men are created equal, that they are endowed by their Creator with certain unalienable rights, that among these are life, liberty and the pursuit of happiness."

In today's solar revolution, leading advocates for energy freedom have urged rooftop solar owners to declare that their rights to make and use their own energy are unalienable and are equal with those of utilities. For example, Jon Wellinghoff, the former chair of the Federal Energy Regulatory Commission, and Steven Weissman, the associate director of the Center for Law, Energy and the Environment, wrote in a 2015 article in the *Energy Law Journal* that:

> Property owners in the United States have the right to generate electricity onsite, for their own use. This understanding is so fundamental that legislatures have not bothered to spell it out. But the right does exist in the law, and it derives both from

> common law principles concerning the beneficial use of property and from federal and state laws that imply that property owners can self-generate through encouragement, protection, or facilitation of such activity.

In June 2017, with Wellinghoff's help, Nevada's legislature passed, and Governor Brian Sandoval signed into law, AB 405, which restored net metering but also recognized the rights of citizens to generate their own power and sell extra power back to their utility at the same retail rate that they would have to buy that power. Solar patriots across the country should work to gain this protection in other states and on the federal level in the future.

In the same spirit and written simply and clearly for an audience of solar homeowners and their allies, Solar United Neighbors, the national group for solar homeowners that we learned about in Chapter 4, published a Solar Bill of Rights in 2017. You can find the full text in Appendix B at the end of this book.

Nine

DIY or Join a Group

The battle, sir, is not to the strong alone;
it is to the vigilant, the active, the brave.

—Patrick Henry

Connecting with a group that supports good public policy for solar will be the easiest way to get started on education, advocacy, and lobbying. But if you're not ready to join a group yet, you can certainly get started on your own.

Lobbying by Yourself

Here's what you'll want to do if you're working solo.

First, educate yourself on the benefits of solar power in terms of energy independence, the environment, job creation, etc. Visit some of the websites or read one of the books listed in the Resources section at the end of this book.

Then, get up to speed on the situation in your state. Find out how your state compares to other states in terms of the amount of solar power already installed and the political environment for solar. You can find out your state's rank for installed solar generating capacity from the Solar Energy Industries Association.

If your state does well—for example, if it's listed in SEIA's top ten solar states—then that's good news. If your state continues its leadership that will be a significant achievement for the future. If your state adds new support for solar, that will be a plus.

However, if your state is not ranked in the top ten for installed solar or is even near the bottom, don't worry. That shows why your help is needed. States have moved up the rankings in the past and your goal should be to help your state catch up in terms of the amount of solar it has installed and the policies needed to encourage—and not discourage—more solar power, especially on rooftops.

Find out about current legislation or rules at the local, state, or federal level to help solar. While the state level has been the most important place for solar policy in the last few years, the other levels of government matter too. For example, on the local side, your city or county can decide to go solar themselves. Or local governments can remove red tape like permitting requirements and fees that make it more difficult for local families and businesses to go solar.

On the national level, the federal government can also do a lot to help solar. But so far, the federal government has moved too slowly and not done enough to help solar or even to create a level playing field for solar to compete fairly in the marketplace against highly subsidized fossil fuels and nuclear power.

In recent years, the federal government's main contribution to spreading solar has been to offer the 30 percent federal investment tax credit for people who install solar equipment. As we discussed, this tax credit is due to start winding down in 2019 and completely expire for homeowners in 2021. After that, businesses will still be able to get the credit, but only at a reduced rate of 10 percent.

The federal government has also helped solar with programs to bring down the cost of solar panels and with scientific research to improve solar panels and batteries.

Unfortunately, the federal government has done little to help level the playing field for solar with fossil fuels and nuclear. As we saw in the chapter about subsidies, the United States still offers many more subsidies to dirty energy like oil and coal than it does to solar and other forms of clean energy.

For solar to take its rightful place as America's leading energy source, solar power will have to become cheaper than dirty energy. The federal government can play a key role in helping correct the energy market for this to happen by charging a tax or fee on carbon emissions. That would raise the price of dirty energy, making coal, oil, and gas have to pay for the right to pollute the Commons — our shared air, waterways, soil, etc.

Economists have liked the idea of a carbon tax or fee for years because it would naturally create more market demand for clean energy from American consumers, helping the solar market to explode. And most Americans would agree that cleaning up your own mess, or paying somebody else to do it, is only fair. At the same time, a carbon fee would make solar and other clean energy relatively less expensive.

And if such a carbon fee is "revenue neutral"—that is, if all the money collected by the fee is returned to American consumers in a dividend check sent to all American adults—then this idea could have enough political support from both Republicans and Democrats to become a reality. You can learn more about this promising idea in Chapter 11. And if you decide to support a carbon fee-and-dividend, then you will want to lobby your federal representatives, both your member of Congress and your two senators, to support it too.

Finally, finish up your research by finding out about proposed government actions that could harm or slow down solar. On the state level, this would include any proposal to let utilities add a fixed charge to the electric bill of solar homeowners. You can do all this research online yourself if you're comfortable with that. And if you want some help, you can subscribe to email alerts from one of the groups listed in Appendix D such as Solar United Neighbors or Vote Solar that will tell you about bills coming up in your state legislature or in Washington, DC that could either help or hurt solar.

Once you feel comfortable that you're familiar with the current solar policy needs in your city or state, start reaching out to government officials. There are several easy ways to begin:

- Reach elected officials indirectly through your local newspaper, which they or their staff read every day. Write letters to the editor urging officials to support better solar policy.
- Contact local officials such as members of your city council, county board of supervisors, or school board asking them to get more solar on local government buildings and make it easier for solar companies to do business in your area.
- Contact offices of federal officials such as your Congressional representative or your two senators. Ask them to support good solar policy in general. Or, if you know about a specific bill that would either help or hurt solar, then give your opinion about that.

Reaching out to government officials can sound scary if you've never done it before. But don't worry. They're used to hearing from citizens on all sorts of issues every day. You pay their salary, so don't be shy about telling them what you think.

Calling officials is effective. With local officials such as city council members, you may get to talk to them directly. With state or national officials such as your state representative or member of Congress, you'll get to talk to a staffer or leave a voice message. Either way, staffers will log your call, tally it with other calls on the same subject, and present a report to the elected official.

I keep the phone number of my two federal senators' and my member of Congress in my mobile phone contacts. That way, I can easily reach their offices when I want to give them my opinion about a bill that I think they'll be considering or voting on soon.

Writing can be even more effective, especially for legislators at the state and federal levels. As Congressional expert Bradford Fitch writes, "Next to having a one-on-one meeting with your congressman, sending an email or letter is the most effective way to influence undecided lawmakers."

Keep in mind that paper letters sent to offices of Congress or the Senate in Washington, DC will have to go through a security screening process. This could delay your letter by a month or more. A faster way to write to your legislators is by email, either directly using your legislator's office email address or through the constituent contact form on the legislator's official website.

Even better is to hand deliver paper letters to a legislator's office. Advocacy groups can help their members with this. For example, Citizen's Climate Lobby offers an "Envoy" system where members of the group who live in the District of Columbia offer to deliver letters, usually in bundles, written by CCL members in other parts of the country to their federal legislators' offices on Capitol Hill. This is just one of the advantages of lobbying with a group rather than on your own, as you'll see below.

And of course, if you can get an in-person meeting with a member of a legislator's staff, or even, if you're very lucky, with the legislator himself or herself, then you've struck gold as a citizen-lobbyist. It's not hard to schedule such a meeting. But it will require you to travel to the official's office, whether in their home district, or in your state capital, or in Washington, DC. And it will be more effective if you're well prepared for how the meeting should go.

Plan to start the meeting on a positive note. Connect with the official at the beginning on something that you both agree about, even if it doesn't have to do with solar power. Then, ask for something specific, such as supporting or opposing a particular bill on solar. Keep it simple and unemotional. Give your reasons in a few short bullet points and share any printed materials you may have brought. Finally, let the official give you his or her take on the issue and ask what it would take for them to agree to your request.

Lobbying with a Group

Communicating with elected officials is one area where working with a group may make it easier for you.

Groups can also help you be more effective. For example, an easy way to connect with officials is to send an email or sign an online petition. Unfortunately, research has shown that such a low-touch method of communication is not particularly effective. Officials pay little attention to form emails or online petitions. Instead, it's more effective to send a personalized email, make a phone call, or write a paper letter. And of course, the most impactful way to communicate with an elected official is to meet with them in person.

You can do all those things on your own if you're motivated enough and if you're comfortable working as a solo player. But especially when it comes to setting up an in-person meeting with a senator or member of Congress, it will be much easier if you work with a group. The group can schedule the meeting for you, send other members to accompany you to the meeting, and even provide you with advice and materials to make your case convincingly for that particular official.

You can certainly form your own group. For example, you can recruit family and friends to get together and make calls. You can even appoint one person from your group to schedule an appointment with an official that your whole group will attend.

However, if you join an existing group that does these things already, then you won't have to search around for people to recruit to help you. You can just tap into the group's list of existing members in your area. You'll also get the benefit of that group's experience, reputation, and educational materials for communicating with elected officials.

And the good news is that there are groups that support solar power from across the political spectrum, from free-market conservatives to people of faith who want to care for God's creation to advocates for solutions to climate change to deep-green environmentalists. You'll probably fall somewhere in between, which is even better news, since most groups out there these days fall in the middle too. The next chapter will help you find a group that supports solar power that will appeal to you.

From the Revolution: Washington Crossing the Delaware

The American Revolution almost ended in failure at several times, but one of the worst was just a few months after the Declaration of Independence was signed. In the summer and fall of 1776, the British beat the Americans in one battle after another. After taking New York City and routing the Americans on Long Island and around the area, the British pursued Washington's army into New Jersey, forcing him to retreat across the Delaware River into Pennsylvania. American civilians started to lose confidence in the patriot cause. Farmers and townspeople alike stopped providing food and shelter to the Continental Army even as an especially cold winter came on.

To save the patriot cause, General George Washington knew he needed a victory on the battlefield. And he was willing to try something desperate to get one. Normally, armies at the time took a break from fighting during the winter. Following this custom, the British and their Hessian allies were preparing to hunker down in their tents and warm themselves around campfires, waiting for the spring to resume fighting. But Washington wasn't willing to wait for the spring.

He decided to attack the New Jersey town of Trenton, occupied by Hessian troops during the winter. To increase his chance of success, Washington planned his attack for the early morning hours of December 26, hoping the Hessians would be sleeping off their Christmas celebrations from the night before. To get to Trenton from his base in Pennsylvania, Washington had to ferry his troops across the Delaware River—in the middle of an especially strong snowstorm. Despite wind, cold, and damp, Washington managed to get 2,400 soldiers and 18 cannons across the river for the early morning attack.

When the Americans arrived in Trenton, it turned out that the Hessians weren't hung over. But they were complacent and unprepared, having called off their night patrols because of the snowstorm. They never bothered to build trenches either, thinking that the Americans were just country clowns who could easily be beaten with bayonets.

As it turned out, the Americans won the day, killing and wounding about 100 Hessians, mortally wounding Hessian commander Johann Rall, and capturing nearly 1,000 others, but losing only seven Americans in the battle. The victory was just what Washington and the patriot cause needed, reigniting support for the rebellion. New soldiers volunteered and farmers started providing food and shelter once again for the Continental troops.

Crossing the Delaware to attack Trenton was a bold and risky move by Washington. But given low public support for his war effort, he knew he had little to lose. Today's solar patriots are in a better position. First, today we know that the public is on our side and that solar is by far America's most popular energy source. Second, we know that we will eventually win and that since its fuel is free and nonpolluting, solar certainly will become America's preferred energy source. It's just a question of when and how that will happen.

The longer the United States waits to get serious about solar, the harder it will be to catch up to other countries and to fight climate change. And if monopoly utilities succeed in locking out most rooftop solar in the future—making the rules favor large solar arrays run by utilities themselves—then our electrical grid will remain vulnerable and inefficient.

That's why rooftop solar advocates need to risk the big battles, just as Washington did when he crossed the Delaware. We should not settle for small gains like keeping net metering in our state. Instead, solar patriots should insist on citizens enjoying full rights to use, share, and sell solar power at fair market value. And we should insist on a national energy marketplace that makes fossil fuels pay their full costs. Only then will solar be as affordable as a clean energy source with no fuel cost and little pollution should be.

Ten

How to Find the Right Group for You

The good men may do separately is small
compared with what they may do collectively.

—Benjamin Franklin

Joining a group, even if it's only remotely via the Internet, is the best way to push for government rules and laws that will help solar power. You'll find two types of groups that support solar policy changes:

- Solar-only groups
- Groups that include solar as one of several issues

Depending on your interests and where you live, one or both types of groups may interest you.

Solar-Only Groups

In the United States, the main groups focused exclusively on solar power tend to be associations of industry professionals such as the Solar Energy Industries Association. Its members are people who work at solar companies. These include firms that manufacture solar panels, inverters, racks, and other equipment for solar power along with businesses that install solar energy systems for homes, businesses, and electric utilities. As SEIA's website puts it, they "represent the entire solar industry; from the small-business owners to the multi-national companies, from the installers on the roof to the engineers in the lab."

Out of self-interest, these companies support a fair marketplace for solar so that they can grow their businesses. Fortunately, that's also what America needs right now to gain clean energy independence.

SEIA does offer some resources about big issues of public policy on solar power. You can see SEIA's top priorities for good solar policy in Appendix C of this book. But since SEIA's information is aimed at solar industry professionals, the average solar homeowner may find it to be a bit dry or technical. Also, critics have accused SEIA of favoring big solar plants owned by utilities over small solar arrays installed on rooftops of homes and small businesses, so some of their information may be less interesting to citizens who support more rooftop solar.

Other groups advocating for solar power may offer more accessible information about solar public policy. On a national level, Vote Solar has been advocating for better solar policy since 2002. As their website puts it, "Vote Solar has worked to remove regulatory barriers and implement key policies needed to bring solar to scale." The group focuses on supporting or opposing legislation in different states, from California to Colorado to Massachusetts, depending on whether the proposed policy will either help or hurt solar power.

For example, in 2017 they ran a campaign to allow community solar (shared solar) in Connecticut:

> **Join Our Fight for Connecticut's Clean Energy Economy.** Right now, Connecticut lawmakers can unlock solar access for all Connecticut families and businesses statewide. A community "shared solar" program will expand access to clean energy choices, lower utility bills, and promote a healthier environment in our communities.

Another national group advocating for good solar policy is Solar United Neighbors, a group mentioned several times in this book and whose clear and powerful Solar Bill of Rights you'll find in Appendix B. Finally, depending on where you live, there may also be a group focused on solar rights for your state or region. For example, where I live in Virginia, solar companies and environmental groups have united with concerned citizens to form the Virginia Distributed Solar Alliance.

Multi-Issue Groups that Include Solar

You may be more attracted to one of the multi-issue groups that also handles solar power.

What's the best way to find a group that's right for you?

First, pick a group that matches your other interests. For example, if you're a person of faith, you might be interested in joining other believers working on behalf of solar power. Examples include Interfaith Power and Light, which welcomes people of all faiths, or groups specific to a particular faith such as the Christian Coalition (rooftop solar is now one of their top issues), the Coalition on the Environment and Jewish Life, or the Buddhist Environmental Initiative.

Or, if your focus is the environment, then you have your choice of several well established national groups, from the Sierra Club to the Natural Resources Defense Council to Greenpeace to 350.org founded by author Bill McKibben to the Climate Reality Project founded by Al Gore. You can also look for local groups focused on the environment or even on climate change, such as the Chesapeake Climate

Action Network covering the mid-Atlantic states. Some groups also combine renewable energy with social issues. For example, Green for All, founded by civil rights leader and former advisor to the Obama White House, Van Jones, works both to spread clean energy and to lift people out of poverty.

People who support free-market principles may like such newer groups as ConservAmerica, Conservatives for Clean Energy, or RepublicEn, the latter founded by former South Carolina Congressman Bob Inglis who we first learned about in Chapter 2. In your local area, there may be a group of conservatives advocating for renewable energy such as the Green Tea Party in Georgia, or the Palmetto Conservative Solar Coalition in South Carolina.

Find the group's website and check out their approach and their accomplishments. Then if the group seems like a good fit for you, make contact. If they have a local chapter in your area, go to their next meeting. If not, then try to talk to a representative of the group by phone or at least by email. Maybe if you get involved enough, you'll end up starting a local chapter!

Not to leave out progressives, but you'll find plenty of likeminded people who also support climate action and rooftop solar in the environmental groups listed earlier, at your local Democratic Party Committee, or in smaller groups that bundle clean energy and environmental protection with such issues as gender and racial equality, labor rights, and building peace.

Groups make it easy for you to connect with them. They'll give you a warm and friendly welcome if you come to one of their meetings. Group organizers are always grateful to connect with potential new members. As a solar homeowner, you'll be especially interesting to any group that's pushing for better solar policy. Most groups don't charge any membership dues. And for those that do, you usually don't need to become a paying member to attend a meeting or two and get started with their outreach efforts in support of solar.

You should also consider the solutions that the group proposes. Is it net metering and other incentives for solar homeowners? Is it different environmental regulations and limits on pollution from fossil fuels? Or tax reform that helps make clean energy more affordable?

One solution popular now with groups that support renewable energy across the political spectrum mentioned earlier is carbon fee-and-dividend. This idea would let the free market decide between fossil fuels and clean energy based on price. Groups including the conservative-leaning Climate Leadership Council and the bi-partisan Citizens' Climate Lobby support this idea as the most powerful way to encourage clean energy. Since this solution has so much promise to help solar, let's look into it a bit in the next chapter.

From the Revolution: French Allies

The American Revolution was a lopsided contest from the start. On one side, representing American patriots, the Continental Army—amateur soldiers straight off the farm, hastily organized into an army so poorly funded that soldiers and suppliers alike were paid in IOUs. On the other side, fighting for King George III, the British Army—professional soldiers of the world's most extensive empire, well-fed, well-armed, well-trained, and backed up by the ships of the British Navy, the world's largest fleet of warships. The Americans may have had the home-field advantage, along with grit and determination. But without the help of powerful allies from abroad, the Americans never could have beat Britain.

France, Spain, and Holland aided the Americans less for sympathy with the ideals of freedom and equality embodied in the Declaration of Independence than to tweak those nations' common enemy, Great Britain. Yet, it was the Americans who got the most benefit.

France in particular helped tip the balance in favor of the Americans. Even before French King Louis XVI declared war on Britain, idealistic and ambitious French officers, including the Marquis de Lafayette, volunteered to help lead American troops, and the French government secretly provided Washington's army with weapons and ammunition. When the French openly entered the war in 1778, their powerful military helped the Americans on both sea and land. The combined American and French forces won their greatest victory at the Battle of Yorktown, which brought the war to a victorious conclusion. We'll discuss Yorktown in the next chapter.

Today's solar homeowners have already teamed up with several key allies in the fight for solar rights against monopoly utilities. Allies have included solar industry trade groups such as the Solar Energy Industries Association and environmental groups such as the Sierra Club. But solar allies are up against a formidable and established opponent. Like the army of King George III, the forces of monopoly utilities are well-funded and well-armed, in their case, with lobbyists and public relations departments. To stand up to the imperial might of utilities, solar patriots need all the help they can get.

In the future, if they can be convinced that rooftop solar is needed along with utility solar, then unlikely allies including some of America's biggest corporations such as Amazon and Microsoft may prove decisive in helping solar homeowners win. It all begins with reaching out to those who may not yet have joined the fight for rooftop solar rights but who clearly have a stake in helping America switch to a clean-energy economy.

Eleven

The New Killer App to Spread Solar

We have it in our power to begin
the world over again.

—Thomas Paine

In the technology world, a killer app is a software program or service that creates its own market. For example, Uber created a new market of people who wanted a ride to work but didn't want to spend the money on a taxi. Likewise, Airbnb created a market for tourists who wanted to stay in private homes.

What would a killer app to spread solar look like? To start with, it might not be a software program or online service. Instead, a killer app for solar might be a new idea in public policy.

Along with a free and unlimited source of fuel—the sun—the main advantage of solar power is that its fuel is clean and doesn't create greenhouse gas pollution. So, any policy that reduces greenhouse gas pollution from energy will also help to spread solar power. That's why a killer app to fight climate change would also be a killer app to spread solar power.

A Solution to Break through the Biggest Barriers

"What we really need is a killer app for climate policy," climate activist Ted Halstead says in a TED Talk video that's started to go viral online. "In the climate world, a killer app is a new solution so promising that it can break through the seemingly insurmountable barriers to progress."

Imagine a policy idea that would let the magic of the marketplace do all the work to spread solar power. Then, imagine if this idea had support from both progressives and conservatives. And what if the idea were easy to understand and simple to implement?

That idea is carbon-fee-and-dividend, according to Halstead, who first encountered the policy from Citizens' Climate Lobby's Marshall Saunders and Mark Reynolds. Since 2007, the group's volunteers have been promoting carbon-fee-and-dividend to Congress and various think tanks. Their work has succeeded in gaining support all across the political spectrum, from conservative Republicans like Halstead, former South Carolina Republican Congressman Bob Inglis whom we've discussed several times in this book, and former Secretary of State George Shultz to progressive Democrats like Senator Sheldon Whitehouse of Rhode Island and former Vice President Al Gore.

These leaders agree that we need to do something new. America has tried regulating climate pollution for years, and it's failed to slow the pace of climate change. Almost invariably, as recent decades have passed without serious action to cut greenhouse gas pollution, the next year is hotter than the last.

The best hope of success may be a simpler approach to cutting pollution from dirty energy that will work with the free market. A carbon fee-and-dividend would encourage businesses and families to use less polluting energy sources by helping the marketplace set more accurate prices for energy and the products and services that use energy.

The carbon-fee-and-dividend proposal suggests putting a fee on carbon pollution at the source—such as a coal mine or an oil or gas well or even a shipping terminal where tankers bring in imported oil—and then returning 100 percent of the proceeds to the American people in the form of a rebate. Under this plan, an average family of four would get a check for about $2,000 initially. Over time, that amount could increase. If the federal government implemented carbon dividends as proposed by the

Climate Leadership Council, seven out of ten American families would get more money back as rebates than they spend on carbon fees priced into the products and services they purchase, according to the U.S. Treasury.[17]

Helping Congress understand that carbon-fee-and-dividend is the "killer app" that will usher the United States into an age of renewable energy independence has been the main work of the volunteers of Citizens' Climate Lobby. Through constituent lobbying and relationship building across party lines, CCL's members have helped form the Climate Solutions Caucus, 62 members strong as of November of 2017. The perfectly bipartisan Congressional caucus is committed to exploring climate actions and solutions, and represents real progress in building political will.

Unlike net metering or the 30 percent federal investment tax credit for solar power equipment, a carbon fee is not specifically designed to help solar power. But a carbon fee will have the effect of boosting all clean energy, including solar power, by making clean energy more affordable relative to fossil fuels.

In various proposals for a carbon fee under discussion recently, the federal government would impose a carbon fee ranging from $15 to $25 or more per ton of carbon dioxide that would be emitted on fossil fuels. A carbon fee would force dirty energy producers to pay for the right to emit carbon pollution, instead of getting to pollute for free, as they have up till now. That fee is key to letting the marketplace decide whether Americans continue to use dirty energy or start to put in more clean energy.

The fee would be paid by companies when they produce or import carbon-based fuels. In turn, those companies would pass the fees along to their customers who use the fuel whether to generate electricity or to run cars, trucks, and planes or even to make plastics and chemicals.

Paying the fee and passing it along to customers would have the effect of making dirty energy and all the things made and transported using fossil fuels more expensive. And that will make clean energy, including solar power, and all the things made and transported with clean energy, cheaper in comparison. Economists and veteran policymakers alike think that a carbon fee will be one of the best ways to help solar spread more quickly across America.

Stronger and More Popular than Solar Subsidies

"The most powerful incentive is going to come when there are economic reasons apparent from our power meters as to why solar makes sense. That's when it's going to really take off," former South Carolina Congressman Bob Inglis told me. "Of course, what we're talking about there is a price on carbon dioxide so we see the true cost of energy. And when we see that in the liberty of enlightened self-interest, consumers will be dialing solar installers without anybody telling them what to do. It's going to change the way we do electricity in this county."

Politically, the best news may be that the general public strongly supports putting a fee on carbon. According to the results of a poll released in September of 2017 by Yale University, a majority of registered voters—roughly 66 percent—support taxing fossil fuel in response to growing threats of climate change.[18] According to the survey, the average American would be willing to spend $177 per year to address climate change, about 14.4 percent more on energy when compared to current electricity rates in each state.

Compared to past policies to encourage solar power, a carbon fee has important advantages:

1. Unlike today's crazy-quilt of clean energy subsidies and incentives, a carbon fee is simple to understand and simple to implement. Studies predict that a steadily rising fee on carbon emissions from fossil fuels would be one of the most effective ways to slow climate change and to speed up clean energy, especially rooftop solar.
2. Today's solar incentives, with a variety of expiration dates, are unpredictable. To make things more confusing, solar incentives vary widely by state. Both of these factors create uncertainty for solar buyers, making it hard for homeowners and solar

installers alike to plan for the future, and to do business in more than one state. If a carbon fee was applied at the federal level, it would be the same in all states. A fee that would increase over a period of decades would provide even more predictability and give people confidence that making an investment in solar today would be good for the future too.

3. A carbon fee with a dividend included might be the most politically viable option to encourage solar today. While Republicans and Democrats fight about climate policy and clean energy incentives, lawmakers and influential leaders from both parties already support a carbon fee-and-dividend.

On the point about politics, a carbon fee that refunds all proceeds to citizens through dividend payments offers a lot to Republicans, who have provided the main opposition to clean energy subsidies in the past. See what Ted Halstead says:

> Although the Republican Party has long been hostile to emissions reductions, a carbon dividends plan offers the GOP several strategic advantages. First, dividends should appeal to the party's base... For the GOP establishment, corrective taxes are fully consistent with free market principles, and

> once firmly in place, justify the elimination of a range of existing regulations, including the Clean Power Plan. The policy's post-partisan appeal stems from the fact that all major factions could claim an important victory.

Carbon-fee-and-dividend could be the killer app to break two decades of partisan gridlock on climate policy and it could do more than any other idea to make solar power more affordable across the United States.

From the Revolution: Battle of Yorktown

With French help, in the summer of 1781, General Washington finally felt that he had the strength to besiege the British in New York and try to take back the city that he'd lost five years earlier. But when French intelligence learned that the leading British General, Lord Charles Cornwallis, had moved up from North Carolina and was heading for Yorktown in Virginia to await supply ships or else evacuate his army by sea, the French urged Washington to change his plans and head south. Washington agreed, but made a feint against British forces in New York to conceal his true plans as he started moving the bulk of Continental forces to Virginia as quietly as possible.

While American and French armies headed south, a French fleet under command of Admiral François de Grasse blocked the entrance to Chesapeake Bay, preventing British ships from supporting or evacuating Cornwallis's army. With the 9,500-man British force trapped at Yorktown, its back to the York River and no way to escape, a combined force of Americans under Washington and French under General Jean Baptiste de Rochambeau began bombarding British positions on October 9.

Eight days later, on October 17, with mounting casualties of 600 dead and wounded, Cornwallis asked the

Americans and French for a cease fire. Then, on October 19 the British signed articles of capitulation that made 8,000 of Cornwallis's soldiers into American prisoners, the largest British army captured during the war.

Several skirmishes took place after Yorktown, but as support for continuing to fight in America evaporated in Britain and pro-war government ministers in London lost their jobs, leaders on both sides of the Atlantic knew that the war was now over. All that was left was to negotiate the peace.

For today's solar patriots, our equivalent of the Battle of Yorktown lies in the future. A final victory for rooftop solar rights could take a variety of forms. That victory could be a carbon-fee-and-dividend that creates a tidal wave of demand for home solar and forces monopoly utilities to finally surrender control of the electric grid to the public. But whatever form the final victory for rooftop solar will take, it must come at the federal level, to cover solar rights for the whole country, and not just in certain lucky states for solar such as California or New York.

In the meantime, many battles will need to be fought in different states, just as Washington's army fought battles in New England or in New York or in Virginia. Solar patriots should celebrate when they win in their state. But they should not get complacent. Winning in your own state is not enough.

Washington's final victory was not won by any one state's militia fighting for that state. Victory at Yorktown was won by the Continental Army fighting for all thirteen original American states. In the same way, the only lasting victory for all Americans to enjoy their rights to clean solar power that they make themselves will happen not in Sacramento or Albany but only in Washington, DC.

Twelve

To Arms!

THESE are the times that try men's souls. The summer soldier and the sunshine patriot will, in this crisis, shrink from the service of their country; but he that stands by it now, deserves the love and thanks of man and woman.

—Thomas Paine

I hope now that you're ready to join the ranks of solar homeowners who are fighting for solar rights. You have good reason to fight, since the cause is your own. If you've already invested in solar panels at home, then you'll want to protect your investment. You'll want to be able to continue to sell extra power back to the grid at a fair rate—without having to pay a high monthly fee or special power rates that discriminate against solar homeowners.

The cause of solar in America is also your own if you care about the future of our country. Getting solar panels was already an important step for you to leave a legacy to future generations. They will praise you for contributing to America's clean energy independence. And today, your leadership can inspire other people to follow your example. As we've seen, the example of a homeowner who's already gone solar is perhaps the most powerful message to encourage neighbors, family, and friends to go solar themselves.

It can be easy to do your part to spread solar among the people you know. Once people find out that you have solar panels at home, many of them will want to know about it. They'll ask you about how much it cost, is it worth it, what incentives are available, what the installation process was like, how you found a solar installer, and other questions about your home solar array. By just answering questions like these as they come up naturally in conversation, you will help to create awareness and interest in solar power.

You can go further by referring your neighbors, family, and friends to your solar installation company. You can do this informally, by just giving your recommendation. Or, if your installer offers a customer referral program, you can become a member. In that way, you might be able to earn referral bonuses when people you know sign up to go solar at their homes. And you might also be able to get help from your solar company in approaching people about going solar. This help can range from the solar company providing you with a fact sheet you can give out to offering you help holding an event at your home or church with refreshments and a speaker.

And if you're ready to do even more to spread solar, you can step up to the role of citizen-lobbyist. You can certainly start contacting public officials to express your support for solar power on your own. But joining a local or national group dedicated to solar or clean energy will make it easier and help your outreach be more effective.

A group can help you find out about proposed actions by local, state, and federal government that might affect solar power in your area. A group can also coach you on making effective contacts with public officials, from members of city council to members of Congress. A group can offer you advice for writing persuasive letters to your local paper. Finally, a group can connect you with new friends who can offer you moral support and encouragement in your outreach as a citizen standing up for solar rights.

If you are serious about lobbying for government regulations and new laws that make it easier for more homeowners to go solar, then I strongly suggest that you join a group. Fortunately, these days you'll find a wide range of groups that support solar appealing to a variety of interests, ranging from the far-left to the far-right on the political spectrum. And of course, everything in between. You're certain to find a group that's for you. Just check out the list of groups in Appendix D of this book.

To be an effective advocate for solar power, you'll need information. Groups and other resources listed in Appendix D can help you find the facts and background you need to become an expert on solar policy. And the list of solar myths busted in Appendix A will help you answer some of the most common challenges you'll hear about whether solar power is viable to power America's economy today.

Information will empower you and give you confidence to speak up for solar as an energy source that's ready to go at this very minute. But just as important as being armed with information is being fired by inspiration.

Spreading solar around America will take decades to complete. It's probably inevitable that our country will run primarily on solar power in the future. But when that happens is up to us. And timing is important. The longer America waits to go solar, the longer we will be stuck in a dirty energy economy that endangers our future. And the longer America waits to take leadership on solar, the more that other nations such as China will gain an advantage over us in creating jobs and installing a new energy system for the 21st century.

Going solar sooner could be what's needed to help America maintain its leadership in the global economy.

It will take advocates like you to help solar come sooner rather than later. And the fight for solar rights will not be an easy war to win. There will be many battles with electric utilities just like those fought in Nevada in 2016 and 2017 over net metering and fixed charges. Other states will become battlefields for overreaching utilities who want to crush solar homeowners just to preserve their monopoly power over energy and keep their profits high for a few more years.

In the short term, solar homeowners must fight to preserve their current solar rights to net metering and to avoid discrimination by electric utilities that want to charge monthly fees or apply special rates only to solar homeowners. These fights will happen primarily at the state level, from California to New York, from Florida to Oregon, from Alaska to Hawaii.

But for the longer term, solar homeowners should start to work on the federal level to pass a national policy that will help solar become America's main energy source. So far, the most promising idea to do that is a carbon fee that would make fossil fuels more expensive and make solar and other clean energy sources cheaper. By helping the free market to set prices more accurately for different types of energy, more Americans will choose solar based entirely on price.

By combining the carbon-fee idea with a dividend that would refund 100 percent of the proceeds to American families equally, this idea will be fair to low-income homeowners and the idea will also be viable politically. Since the refund would make a carbon fee different than a tax, Congress is more likely to pass a carbon fee that's coupled with a dividend. This is the idea that both Republicans including former Secretaries of State George Shultz and James A. Baker III and Democrats such as Al Gore support.

Victory in Sight

To win battles to protect solar rights in the short term and to gain a fair market for rooftop solar power in the long term, the solar industry needs an army of solar homeowners who will stand up for solar rights. Just as King George III brought the world's most powerful military machine to bear upon the American patriots after they declared their independence from imperial rule in 1776, so today's electric utilities come to battles with solar homeowners heavily armed with lobbyists and with an army of mercenaries (like the fake citizens group Consumers for Smart Solar that pushed the anti-solar Amendment 1 in 2016) ready to fight to preserve their rule.

Beating these energy tyrants with the people power of energy patriots will take patience and perseverance. It will also take the vigilance and nimbleness showed by Paul

Revere in his midnight ride to warn the towns of Lexington and Concord that the British were coming.

So, just as Thomas Paine said that fighting for American freedom from King George III was not for *summer soldiers and sunshine patriots*, so the fight for solar rights will not be easy or quick. But like the ordinary citizens who fought as soldiers in the American Revolution, those citizens who fight the solar revolution today will deserve the thanks of all Americans today and for generations to come.

After Victory, Making Peace with Utilities

To be fair, not all electric utilities are energy tyrants. Some utilities, especially in California and New York, have been working with the solar industry to integrate more solar into the grid for years. And these responsible utilities have also been trying to fairly reward solar homeowners for the extra clean solar power that they sell back to the grid to share with their neighbors.

Whether utilities work positively with solar homeowners today or utilities continue to try to exercise monopoly control over the electricity in their territory, nobody will benefit by crushing utilities. With a century of experience keeping the lights on, utilities have an important place in America's clean energy future.

The question is: how to best use utilities' expertise and vast resources to put the interests of the American people ahead of the private interests of utility shareholders and CEOs?

As long as utilities own the wires that connect your house with extra solar power to sell to other homes that need solar power, utilities will have a financial incentive to find ways to block access of solar homeowners to the grid so they can sell more power from the big power plants that they operate themselves.

Consider an example that may be familiar to the ordinary person: watching TV shows on the Internet.

Verizon or Comcast may provide your Internet service. But they don't also produce the streaming shows you watch online such as *Game of Thrones* or *Stranger Things*. And that's a very good thing. Because if Internet service providers not only sold you Internet service but also produced their own TV shows, then those ISPs would have a business interest in blocking other TV shows from their Internet service. If ISPs made their own content and distributed it over their own wires, that would mean you could have plenty of "World Headlines from Verizon" or "Comcast Comedy Hour," but less of CNN or Comedy Central.

It's the same with electric utilities and the electrical grid. If utilities control not just the wires, but also offer their own power, then they have a business interest in blocking other power providers, including solar homeowners, from selling power on the utilities' own grid. That's called a conflict of interest.

To eliminate the utilities' conflict of interest and provide fair access to the grid to rooftop solar owners, it will be necessary to "decouple" or separate the two functions of a) producing power and b) running the electrical grid.

Running the grid together with power plans was necessary in the old days, when utilities were the only ones able to produce electric power. But it's not necessary today for the same company to both run the grid and produce power when homeowners and other small producers can also make their own electricity.

"Structure the rules for the market and rules for the utility system based on today, not on 100 years ago," John Farrell, who serves as Director of Energy Democracy at the Institute for Local Self-Reliance told me.

Updating our electricity system's rules would involve decoupling power production from controlling the grid.

The most common idea for decoupling is to let utilities continue to run the grid, while making them spin off their power plants to other companies. If you'd like to know more about this idea, check out the Alliance to Save Energy, which explains how this type of decoupling can help encourage more solar but can also get utilities on board to help their customers use less energy overall through conservation and efficiency.

A more radical version of decoupling involves the opposite: let utilities continue to run big power plants, but take away their power over the electrical grid. John Farrell at ILSR favors this approach.

To give solar homeowners a fair way to sell power to other people who want to use solar but don't have their own, Farrell thinks that we should put the grid in the hands of a non-profit organization that doesn't also produce electricity.

That grid operator would then solicit competitive bids to provide electricity from all sources fairly. This would finally create a level playing field for solar homeowners with utilities. It would also encourage utilities to update old grid technology to better accommodate rooftop solar producers and help all Americans to use electricity more efficiently.

"The grid has been built like a 40-lane freeway so that you'd never have congestion," Farrell explained. "That was the only way we knew to do it in the past. What we've never thought about is how can we ask the people who are driving to use less power or generate their own lane by bringing their own electricity."

Such an open grid could be just what's needed to give solar homeowners fair access to America's electricity infrastructure. Creating an independent grid could be the peace treaty that's needed for utilities and solar homeowners to finally get along. A firm and fair understanding between solar homeowners and utilities could lead to decades of growth for solar in this century and a more stable electrical grid for everybody's benefit.

It's not about getting rid of electric utilities. It's just about establishing the correct relationship between utilities on the one hand and people who produce distributed solar power on the other. That relationship should not be one of subservience, where monopoly utilities have all the power and will use it to discriminate against rooftop solar owners. Instead, the relationship between utilities and the homeowner and small businesses who make clean energy from rooftop solar needs to be one of equality. Only then can the American people live in peace with electric utilities.

From the Revolution: Treaty of Paris

On September 3, 1783, two years after the Battle of Yorktown, an American delegation of John Adams, Benjamin Franklin, and John Jay met in Paris to sign a peace treaty with David Hartley, an envoy of King George III. The Treaty of Paris formally ended the Revolutionary War. But the accord's significance went beyond Britain recognizing the independence of the United States.

"The Treaty of Paris was a part of the future rather than the past," argues historian Michael Lee Lanning. That's because the Battle of Yorktown had ended the war on the ground. Effectively, the American and French victory at Yorktown had already granted independence to the thirteen former British colonies from New Hampshire in the north to Georgia in the south. The treaty just put that reality on paper.

The real importance of the Treaty of Paris was that it wound up giving the Americans much more land than they had before. The negotiations doubled the size of the new nation, granting the U.S. generous territory well beyond the original Atlantic seaboard states, encompassing new lands extending to the Great Lakes in the north, the Mississippi River in the west, and the Gulf Coast in the south.

The lesson for today's solar patriots is that we should aim high. We should not settle for little victories in our own states such as preserving incentives like net metering or fighting off discriminatory fees like monthly fixed charges on electric bills. Instead, we should keep fighting—and negotiating—until the playing field for rooftop solar is totally level with other energy sources. Only then can solar take its rightful place as America's #1 energy source, with much of that solar capacity located on home rooftops.

For that, solar homeowners will need to work with utility companies. The Treaty of Paris can provide a good lesson for how enemies can become friends, once a proper relationship is established between the two.

Ever since the American victory forced Britain to recognize the United States as an independent nation in 1783, the two nations have enjoyed a connection so close that diplomats refer to it as the "Special Relationship." And after the War of 1812, the United States never fought another war against Great Britain. Instead, the two nations became the strongest of allies, fighting side by side in both World Wars and enjoying strong trade, cultural exchange, and tourism.

In the same way, once solar homeowners and their allies force utilities to abandon their monopoly on producing power and agree to respect the rights of solar homeowners to freely access America's electrical grid, then solar patriots and electric utilities can become good friends. Both parties can work together to make sure that America enjoys clean, reliable electricity for decades to come.

Appendices

Appendix A: Top Ten Myths about Rooftop Solar Busted

Facts are stubborn things; and whatever may be our wishes, our inclinations, or the dictates of our passions, they cannot alter the state of facts and evidence.

—John Adams

If you have solar on your home, you already know that it's affordable, practical, and clean. But too many Americans still believe that solar isn't ready for prime time or that it actually hurts the environment. This list of solar myths, with answers for each, will help you bust these myths as you talk to people you know about solar power. If you decide to step up as a citizen-lobbyist for solar policy, the list will also help you talk to public officials.

Myth #1: Solar Power is Too Expensive: Traditional sources of electricity such as natural gas and nuclear power are cheaper.

Fact: The price of solar decreased 80 percent between 2008 and 2013, according to the GW Solar Institute. As more people go solar, mass production will cause the costs of solar to fall even further. Meanwhile, the cost to buy electricity from utilities that sell a mix of power primarily from fossil fuels and nuclear power has remained nearly steady for the last decade. Regulations on pollution are sure to raise the cost of dirty energy in the future. Removing high taxpayer subsidies for coal, oil, gas, and nuclear power would further raise the price of dirty energy and make solar relatively cheaper.

Myth #2: Solar Power isn't Practical Yet: A large industrial economy like that of the United States cannot rely yet on solar power as its main energy source.

Fact: At the turn of the 21st century there were only a thousand solar installations across the country. Today, that number has grown to more than a million. In its best-case scenario, the International Energy Agency projects the U.S. could install 305 gigawatts of solar by 2030 and 737 gigawatts by 2050.[19] That's more than a 1,000 percent increase over 14 years from today's capacity of 27.2 gigawatts. While ambitious, Bloomberg New Energy Finance projects that the country will have 288 gigawatts of solar by 2030, which would put us well on the way to reaching the IEA's ambitious goal. Meanwhile, the Solutions Project and other activist groups are campaigning for the United States to use 100 percent clean energy by 2050. More than half of that clean energy could come from solar power.

Myth #3: Solar Power Can't Provide Energy 24/7: Just as wind turbines only produce power when the wind is blowing, so solar panels only generate electricity when the sun is shining. On cloudy days, solar panels don't work well and at night, they don't work at all. So, we need to turn to traditional energy sources for reliable electricity that's always on.

Fact: It's true that solar panels only generate power when it's light outside. But with new battery technology that's more powerful and more affordable than in the past, it's now practical to store solar power produced during the daytime for use at night. Every year, more people install solar + battery storage. In the state with the most expensive electricity, Hawaii, it already makes financial sense to use batteries instead of buying power from a utility. And if homeowners and small businesses with solar + storage are fairly compensated for the benefits that storage brings to the grid in the future, then more people will install batteries to store their solar power.

Myth #4: America's Electric Grid Can't Handle More Solar Power: To operate reliably, the grid requires a large supply of "baseload" power from large power plants that's always on, the electric grid can only accept a small portion of power from home producers of solar.

Fact: Even without any upgrades, today's Eastern U.S. grid could safely handle up to 30 percent renewable energy, according to the National Renewable Energy Laboratory.[20] In the future, "smart grid" technology that

that can effectively handle power flows not just from the power company to our homes, but also back from our homes to the power company, will be able to accept a majority of its power from renewables including solar.

Myth #5: Solar Panels are Bad for the Environment: Solar panels take up valuable land that can be used for farming or open space. Making solar panels pollutes air and water, while both making and shipping solar panels emits greenhouse gases.

Fact: It's true that large ground-mounted solar plants, as favored by utilities, do use up land. But most small-scale solar is placed on rooftops that aren't being used for anything else. Solar can even help insulate those roofs from sun, rain, and snow, making roofs cooler and helping them last longer. Some solar is also installed in canopies over parking lots or decks, turning unused space into valuable shaded parking. As to their materials, at the end of their lifespan of 25-40 years, 90 percent of the materials from solar panels can be recycled. The clean energy from solar panels offsets their carbon footprint in four years, according to Greenpeace.[21]

Myth #6: Solar Power Can't Survive on Its Own without Government Subsidies: When Solyndra went bankrupt in 2011, the federal government had to write off $139 million of the $192 million loan that the

U.S. Department of Energy made to the solar panel manufacturer. This shows that solar can't compete with traditional energy sources in a free market.

Fact: The loan program involved was actually a success overall. Most of the other companies successfully paid back their loans. Solyndra was also not a typical solar company, but a high-risk startup. Hundreds of other solar companies have found profitable markets making equipment and installing solar panels across the country. Meanwhile, traditional energy sources also heavily rely on government subsidies, and long have. Over the period of time they've been subsidized, fossil fuels and nuclear power have gotten many times more subsidies over time than solar has, according to a 2011 study by DBL Investors. And when you average that out per year, all renewable energy (including solar with wind and others) has cost about $395 million per year. Nuclear power, subsidized for a much longer period, has averaged $3.57 billion annually. But the winner by far for government subsidies is oil and gas, getting an average of $4.91 billion in government subsidies *per year.*

Myth #7: Solar Power Doesn't Work in Cold Climates: Solar panels only produce enough power in sunny places like Arizona, California, or Florida. In northerly states, there's just not enough sun to make solar power worthwhile.

Fact: There's enough sun in every U.S. state to make solar power practical. As proof, consider that the world's fourth-ranking country for solar in 2016, Germany, has sunshine comparable to the state of Alaska. Yet, Germany had more solar capacity installed than the whole United States. So, more important than sunshine is good public policy to encourage the spread of solar, as in the case of Germany. Good solar policy has helped to make some northern states, including New York and New Jersey, leaders in solar, actually helping them to long outrank sunny Florida, which has superior sunshine but has suffered from weak support for solar from state government.

Myth #8: Nuclear Power is Cheaper than Solar: America's coming "Nuclear Renaissance" will build power plants with new technology that will be cheaper than solar.

Fact: After much fanfare, the long-promised nuclear renaissance has never materialized and doesn't look likely to. Several utilities, especially in Georgia and South Carolina, have put plans to expand existing nuclear plants or build new ones on hold after massive cost overruns. Like all traditional sources of energy, nuclear power receives much more money in government subsidies than solar. Even so, nuclear power plants are too expensive to build in today's economy. And when you take out subsidies for both nuclear and solar, nuclear is a much more expensive way to generate electricity. Per megawatt hour, the average utility company can produce electricity with solar as low as $49, while it costs at least $97 to produce the same amount of electricity with nuclear power, according to a 2016 report by investment bank Lazard.[22] That makes nuclear about twice as expensive as solar.

Myth #9: The Best Power Stations Are Big Ones: The cheapest and most reliable electricity will be produced as it has for more than a century, by big power plants run by electric utilities. Solar plants built by utilities can produce power for half the cost of solar panels located on the rooftops of homes. That makes utility solar better.

Fact: It's true that utilities benefit from bulk discounts to buy solar panels cheaply to build large solar farms. But home solar systems offer benefits to their owners and to their neighbors not available from big solar plants. Big centralized solar plants offer tempting targets for terrorists who wouldn't bother targeting thousands of small arrays distributed on homes over a large area. You also lose energy sending power from big solar farms over power lines to the homes who use that power. Finally, solar panels on their own rooftops offer homeowners energy independence that they don't get by relying on their utility company to sell them solar power. Through solar cooperatives run by such organizations as Solar United Neighbors (sometimes also called Solarize programs), homeowners can save 15% or more on the cost of a solar installation by banding together with their neighbors to qualify for a bulk discount.

Myth #10: Solar Homeowners Are Freeloaders Who Don't Pay Their Fair Share to Use the Electric Grid: Solar homeowners who are connected to the electrical grid enjoy the benefits of the grid to back up their solar systems on the one hand. But solar homeowners who zero out their electric bills don't pay any of the costs to maintain the grid on the other hand. Those grid costs are passed along in higher utility rates to their neighbors who don't have solar, which is unfair.

Fact: Solar homeowners provide power to the grid that's about 50 percent more valuable than the credit they get from their utility company. On average, solar homeowners get about 12 cents per kilowatt hour for power they sell to their utility company. But the solar power they produce provides about 17 cents per kilowatt hour worth of benefits to the electrical grid, according to a 2015 report by Environment America based on studies by utility regulators in a dozen states.[23]

By reducing the need for utilities to purchase more traditional fuels and build new power plants, solar homeowners help make electricity cheaper for their neighbors who don't yet have solar. And by offering distributed power that's not subject to blackouts caused by the breakdown of big power plants, solar homeowners make the electricity supply more reliable for their neighbors too.

Appendix B: Solar Bill of Rights (Solar United Neighbors)

Published in 2017 by Solar United Neighbors, a national organization that has been helping solar owners and supporters fight for their energy rights since 2007.

We, the undersigned, believe we have the right to produce our own power.

- We have the right to put solar on our roofs, in our yards, or to share a nearby solar array with our neighbors.
- We have the right to manage our own electricity production and consumption so that we can all save money.
- Solar power creates local jobs, keeps money in our community, makes us more resilient, and enhances our energy security.
- Solar should be affordable and accessible for all.

We believe utilities work for the people—not the other way around.

- Utilities should enable us to take control of our energy—not prevent us from doing so.

- Utilities have an obligation to help the communities they serve transition to clean, locally-produced energy.
- Utilities should not put punitive or arbitrary charges, fees, or rules in the way of solar.

We envision a clean, equitable energy system that directs control and benefits back to local communities, with solar on every roof and money in every pocket.

We're a community of people building a new energy system, and rooftop solar is the cornerstone.

Solar equals energy freedom. Join us today!

You can sign the Solar Bill of Rights at http://www.solarunitedneighbors.org/get-involved-with-solar-united-neighbors/advocate-for-solar/sign-the-solar-bill-of-rights/

Appendix C: Recommended Policies to Encourage Rooftop Solar (SEIA)

The Solar Energy Industries Association recommends policies in seven areas for state governments to encourage rooftop solar, that is, solar installed on site by homeowners, small businesses, and communities for their own use.

Net Metering
Local Permitting
Property-Assessed Clean Energy
Rebates & Incentives
Solar Access Rights
Utility Rate Structure
Grid Modernization

Find out what specific public policy ideas SEIA recommends in each area online at https://www.seia.org/initiative-topics/rooftop-solar

Appendix D: Resources

Groups

The groups listed below advocate for better solar policy at the national level and in various states.

Solar-Specific Groups

Solar United Neighbors: Especially for solar homeowners who want to help spread solar in their communities and beyond. Formerly the Community Power Network, SUN is a coalition of grassroots, local, state, and national organizations working to build and promote locally based renewable energy projects and policies.

Vote Solar: Vote Solar is a non-profit organization working to foster economic opportunity, promote energy security, and fight climate change by making solar a mainstream energy resource. They work at the state level all across the country to support the policies and programs needed to repower our grid with sunshine.

Solar Energy Industries Association: SEIA is the voice of the solar industry at the federal and state level, advocating for the protection and expansion of the U.S.

market for all solar technologies. They represent the entire solar industry; from the small-business owners to the multi-national companies, from the installers on the roof to the engineers in the lab.

Regional: Solar CitiSuns represent homeowners with solar panels working for better public policy in California and Colorado. Groups focusing on other regions or states can be found online.

Renewable Energy and Environment Groups

Citizens' Climate Lobby: Aims to create the political will for climate solutions by "Enabling individual breakthroughs in the exercise of personal and political power." By building constructive, working relationships with members of Congress they seek passage of carbon-fee-and-dividend, a climate change solution that bridges the partisan divide and promises to be more effective than traditional approaches to carbon regulation.

Climate Reality Project: Founded by Al Gore, the group's mission is to catalyze a global solution to the climate crisis by making urgent action a necessity across every level of society. Supports making countries including the United States honor our commitments under the 2015 Paris Climate Agreement.

League of Conservation Voters: LCV, in collaboration with state LCV partners, advocates for sound environmental laws and policies, holds elected officials accountable for their votes and actions, and elects pro-environment candidates who will champion their priority issues. Their top issue is climate change, including clean energy.

Sierra Club: The nation's oldest and largest environmental group, the Sierra Club runs several campaigns, including Ready for 100, promoting America's switch to 100 percent clean energy.

Local Groups: Most areas have chapters of national groups like the Sierra Club or else independent groups focused on local conservation issues or even on climate action for a certain region, such as the Chesapeake Climate Action Network in the mid-Atlantic area.

Especially for Conservatives

Conservative Energy Network: CEN was launched in 2016 by conservatives, for conservatives, to support and connect state-based conservative clean energy and energy efficiency organizations throughout the nation.

Young Conservatives for Energy Reform: This new group seeks to bring together young professional, socially conservative, leaders from across the country in a grassroots effort to influence energy reform and to build and strengthen regional and state coalitions through targeted meetings, press releases, and local media outreach efforts.

RepublicEn: Members of RepublicEn are conservatives, libertarians, and pragmatists of diverse political opinion. "Climate change is real and we believe it's our duty and our opportunity to reduce the risks. But to make a difference, we have to fight climate change with free enterprise instead of ineffective subsidies and regulations."

Regional: Conservatives for Clean Energy supports renewables in North Carolina and Virginia. Led by powerhouse activist Debbie Dooley, The Green Tea Coalition started in Georgia but has expanded into Florida and other southeastern states.

Books

Solar Power and Public Policy

Let It Shine: The 6,000-Year Story of Solar Energy by John Perlin. Foreword by Amory B. Lovins, cofounder and chief scientist of the Rocky Mountain Institute.

Rooftop Revolution: How Solar Power Can Save our Economy—and our Planet—from Dirty Energy by Danny Kennedy. Foreword by General Wesley Clark, US Army (ret.).

Solar Revolution: The Economic Transformation of the Global Energy Industry by Travis Bradford.

Lobbying and Dealing with Government

Citizen's Handbook to Influencing Elected Officials: Citizen Advocacy in State Legislatures and Congress by Bradford Fitch.

America The Owner's Manual: You Can Fight City Hall—and Win by Senator Bob Graham and Chris Hand.

History of the American Revolution

1776 by David McCullough.

The American Revolution: A History by Gordon S. Wood.

The American Revolution 100: The People, Battles, and Events of the American War for Independence, Ranked by their Significance by Michael Lee Lanning.

Washington's Spies: The Story of America's First Spy Ring by Alexander Rose.

Notes

1. "Debate over solar rates simmers in the Nevada desert," PBS NewsHour, published on Feb. 27, 2016. Available online at https://www.pbs.org/newshour/show/debate-over-solar-rates-simmers-in-the-nevada-desert.

2. Orwell, George. *Nineteen Eighty-Four.* Signet Classic, 1961.

3. Sheppard, Kate. "This Messaging Guru Is Helping Utilities Clean Up Their Appearance," *Huffington Post,* published on April 1, 2016. Available online at https://www.huffingtonpost.com/entry/messaging-utilities-solar-power_us_56f45cd6e4b014d3fe22b572.

4. Stumo-Langer, Nick. "Changing the Language of Renewable Energy, the Electric Monopoly's Newest Ploy," Institute for Local Self-Reliance Blog, published on August 18, 2016. Available online at https://ilsr.org/changing-the-language-of-renewable-energy-the-electric-monopolys-newest-ploy/.

5. Kuckro, Rod. "Utilities rebuild an aging lexicon to keep pace with change," E&E News, published on July

6, 2016. Available online at https://www.eenews.net/stories/1060039811.

6. "Insider Reveals Deceptive Strategy behind Florida's Solar Amendment," Miami Herald, published on October 18, 2016. Available online at http://www.miamiherald.com/news/politics-government/election/article109017387.html.

7. Muro, Mark and Devashree Saha. "Rooftop solar: Net Metering is a Net Benefit," Brookings Institution, published on May 23, 2016. Available online at https://www.brookings.edu/research/rooftop-solar-net-metering-is-a-net-benefit/.

8. "Electric Cars and Cheap Solar 'Could Halt Fossil Fuel Growth by 2020'," *The Guardian,* published on February 2, 2017. Available online at https://www.theguardian.com/environment/2017/feb/02/electric-cars-cheap-solar-power-halt-fossil-fuel-growth-2020.

9. Williams, Katie Bo and Cory Bennett. "Why a Power Grid Attack is a Nightmare Scenario," *The Hill*, published on May 30, 2016. Available online at http://thehill.com/policy/cybersecurity/281494-why-a-power-grid-attack-is-a-nightmare-scenario.

10. "How Americans Make Energy Decisions and the Sources and Channels They Trust the Most," 2016 Makovsky Energy Report. Available online at http://www.makovsky.com/wp-content/uploads/2016/09/Makovsky-EnergyReport-FINAL.pdf.

11. Zycher, Benjamin. "Solar Energy Can't Survive without Massive Subsidies," *The Hill,* published on October 26, 2016. Available online at http://thehill.com/blogs/pundits-blog/energy-environment/302900-solar-energy-cant-survive-without-massive-subsidies.

12. "Average U.S. Residential Solar PV Prices," GW Solar Institute at George Washington University. Available online at https://solar.gwu.edu/q-a/will-solar-pv-prices-continue-decline.

13. Johnson, Jeff. "Long History of U.S. Energy Subsidies: Report Shows Centuries of Government Support for Fossil Fuels, Much Less for Renewable Energy," *Chemical and Engineering News*, published on December 9, 2011. Available online at https://cen.acs.org/articles/89/i51/Long-History-US-Energy-Subsidies.html.

14. "True Cost of Gasoline? Try $15 a Gallon," Think Progress, published on June 22, 2011. Available online at

https://thinkprogress.org/true-cost-of-gasoline-try-15-a-gallon-832db0342a70/.

15. "How Much Are We Paying for a Gallon of Gas?" Institute for the Analysis of Global Security. Available online at http://www.iags.org/costofoil.html.

16. "The True Cost of Electricity: What We're Not Paying for Through Our Utility Bills," Environmental Defense Fund Blog, published on April 28, 2016.

17. Horowitz, John, etal, "Methodology for Analyzing a Carbon Tax" U.S. Treasury Office of Tax Analysis, published January 2017. Available online at https://www.treasury.gov/resource-center/tax-policy/tax-analysis/Documents/WP-115.pdf.

18. "US Public Backs Carbon Tax, and Spending Revenue on Renewables," Phys.org, published on September 12, 2017. Available online at https://phys.org/news/2017-09-carbon-tax-revenue-renewables.html.

19. Unger, David J. "America Now Has 27.2 Gigawatts of Solar Energy: What Does That Mean?" *Inside Climate News*, published on May 25, 2016. Available online at https://insideclimatenews.org/news/24052016/

solar-energy-27-gigawatts-united-states-one-million-rooftop-panels-climate-change-china-germany.

20. Timmer, John. "New Analysis Shows Eastern U.S. can Handle 30 Percent Renewable Electricity," *Ars Technica*, published on August 30, 2016. Available online at https://arstechnica.com/science/2016/08/new-analysis-shows-eastern-us-can-handle-30-percent-renewable-electricity/.

21. "Renewable Energy Myths: 6 Myths about Renewable Energy Blown Away," Greenpeace. Available online at http://www.greenpeace.org/international/en/campaigns/climate-change/energyrevolution/renewable-energy-myths/.

22. "Levelized Cost of Energy Analysis 10.0," Lazard, published on December 15, 2016. Available online at https://www.lazard.com/perspective/levelized-cost-of-energy-analysis-100/.

23. "Shining Rewards: The Value of Rooftop Solar Power for Consumers and Society," Environment America, published on October 18, 2016. Available online at https://environmentamerica.org/reports/ame/shining-rewards.

Acknowledgements

Deep gratitude to my wife and best business partner Lindsay who did many things to help this book. She encouraged me to write it in the first place, she discussed it with me along the way, she edited the manuscript, she developed the cover, and she worked with the publisher on layout and printing. Thanks to all the solar companies who've been my clients over the years and to all the homeowners who've fought valiantly for solar rights. I also learned much about advocacy and lobbying from dedicated activists with such groups as the Sierra Club and Citizens' Climate Lobby. Finally, I'd like to thank the talented actor-interpreters at one of my favorite places on earth, Colonial Williamsburg, who inspired me to get into the history of the American Revolution, especially Bill Barker as an older Thomas Jefferson, Kurt Smith as young Jefferson, Ron Carnegie as George Washington, Richard Schumann as Patrick Henry, Katharine Pittman as young Martha Washington, Bryan Austin as James Madison, and James Ingram as African-American Baptist preacher Gowan Pamphlet.

About the Author

The Solar Patriot is Erik Curren's third book and his second one about solar power. With his wife Lindsay, known as Mrs. Solar Patriot, Erik runs the Curren Media Group, which provides marketing services to the solar industry. He is also an experienced advocate and citizen-lobbyist for climate change, clean energy, and solar power on the federal, state, and local levels. As a two-term member of the city council of his current hometown, Staunton, Virginia, Erik gained experience of how government works from the standpoint of an elected official. He's a big history buff and has enjoyed learning about the American Revolution over the last couple years. He and Lindsay enjoy wearing their eighteenth-century costumes to visit historic sites around the Old Dominion from Colonial Williamsburg to Mount Vernon and Monticello and even walking the National Mall in Washington, DC.

76706630R00132

Made in the USA
Middletown, DE
15 June 2018